# FIVE MONTHS IN THE HIMALAYA

# FIVE MONTHS IN THE HIMALAYA

## A RECORD OF MOUNTAIN TRAVEL IN GARHWAL AND KASHMIR

ARNOLD LOUIS MUMM

GYAN

*Published by*

Gyan Publishing House
5, Ansari Road
Daryaganj, New Delhi-110002
Phone: 011-47034999, 9811692060
E-mail: books@gyanbooks.com

*Distribution Network*
gyanbooks.com
India, USA, Canada, UK, Australia



ISBN: 978-93-7447-139-5 (PB)

First Published, 1909

2nd Impression 2026

*Printed at:* Gyan Press, Delhi.



**FIVE MONTHS IN THE HIMALAYA**
Author: ARNOLD LOUIS MUMM

# FIVE MONTHS IN THE HIMALAYA

TRISUL FROM THE SOUTH-WEST.

# FIVE MONTHS IN THE HIMALAYA

## A RECORD OF MOUNTAIN TRAVEL IN GARHWAL AND KASHMIR

BY

A. L. MUMM

LATE HONORARY SECRETARY OF THE ALPINE CLUB

*WITH ILLUSTRATIONS AND MAPS*

LONDON

EDWARD ARNOLD

Publisher to the India Office

1909

# PREFACE

I HAD the good fortune, the year before last, to travel for five months in the Himalaya under exceptionally favourable conditions; over three months were spent in Garhwal and Kumaon, more than six weeks in and about Kashmir. A good deal of hitherto untrodden ground was traversed in both regions, and a large extent of country, of great interest to mountaineers, was visited, which has never been adequately described from their point of view, and never before come under the fire of a camera.

The mountainous portion of Garhwal and Kumaon, which forms a section of the great parallel ranges of the Himalayan chain, contains not only the highest summit, but the largest and finest field for combined climbing and exploration, in British territory; and in Nanda Devi, the summit referred to, and the mountains surrounding it, possesses a group which, for individuality and striking and characteristic features of configuration and structure, may challenge comparison with any in the world. Its natural attractions gain an additional interest from the fact that the whole country is of immemorial sanctity, and was the scene of the marriage of Siva, and many other capital events of the theogony of Brahminism.

Some charming chapters have been devoted to this region by Anglo-Indian sportsmen, but in its mountaineering aspect it has not yet, so far as I am aware, been the subject of a book in the English language. Our sojourn there was signalised by the ascent by four members of the party, of a peak considerably over 23,000 feet in height—a feat which has only been accomplished three or four times at the outside.

Mount Haramukh in Kashmir is of course familiar to hundreds of people, but the range of mountains which separates Kashmir from Khagan, though it can be reached in three days or less, not only from the Vale of Kashmir, but also from Abbottabad or Rawal Pindi, is still almost unknown ground to every one except Major Bruce, and what he has written of it fills barely two pages of the *Alpine Journal.*

The foregoing statement embodies my excuses for adding another to the multitude of books on mountain travel. I should hardly have ventured on such a step if I had not been in a position to illustrate it with some approach to completeness, and I should not have thought of it for a moment if there had been any chance of the thing being done by either of my companions. The book ought, of course, to have been written by one or other of them. Major Bruce stands quite alone as the explorer of the Khagan range, and it is entirely due to him that I was able to see so much of it in so short a time; while it may be safely said that no one person has ever possessed so complete a mountaineering knowledge of an equally large tract of the Himalaya as Dr. Longstaff possesses of Garhwal and Kumaon. I am glad to know that he does purpose writing a detailed narrative of his climbing exploits there and elsewhere, but I have not thought it necessary to take this intention into account, as he only contemplates giving the volume to the world some five-and-twenty or thirty years hence. In the meantime, I have borrowed from him freely, using his map, and about fifteen of his photographs (they are marked with his initials in the List of Illustrations), and drawing largely on his articles in the *Alpine* and *Geographical Journals*. The latter proceeding was to some extent rendered compulsory by the fact that I did not take part in the principal expeditions accomplished in Garhwal, but my debt to him in this respect is much heavier than appears on the surface, and extends far beyond the extracts which are indicated as such by inverted commas.

Yet, though I have borrowed without scruple, this part of the story must inevitably suffer from being told by the least active member of the party ; on the other hand, there may be some value in a candid record of the impressions, agreeable and the reverse, of one who is well past his mountaineering prime, and was at no time endowed with a physique or mountaineering powers of an exceptional kind.

And now, my last word must be one of grateful recognition of unnumbered kindnesses from every one of our company, travellers, guides, and Gurkhas, all of whom were united in the bonds of a most pleasant and harmonious comradeship. To them, not less than to the beauties and sublimities of Nature, it is due that the memory of this journey is a possession beyond all price. I should like to think that a little of the charm and joy of it has found its way into the following pages.

A. L. M.

*March* 1909.

# CONTENTS

## CHAPTER I



## CHAPTER II



## CHAPTER III



## CHAPTER IV



## CHAPTER V



## CHAPTER VI



## CHAPTER VII



## CHAPTER VIII



## CHAPTER IX

# FIVE MONTHS IN THE HIMALAYA

# LIST OF ILLUSTRATIONS

# LIST OF ILLUSTRATIONS

## LIST OF ILLUSTRATIONS



### MAPS

# FIVE MONTHS IN THE HIMALAYA

## CHAPTER I

### INTRODUCTORY

IN 1905 Lord Curzon, who was then Viceroy of India, wrote a letter to Mr. Douglas Freshfield suggesting that it was time that the exploration of Mount Everest should be undertaken by a competent party under the auspices of the Royal Geographical Society and the Alpine Club, and making a most generous offer of assistance on behalf of the Indian Government.[1] Nothing came of this at the moment, and Lord Curzon left India soon afterwards, but the letter naturally made a considerable stir in mountaineering circles; in particular it attracted the attention of Major the Hon. C. G. Bruce, of the 5th Gurkha Rifles, and thereby brought about the journey which is described in the following pages.

It was said years ago by a competent authority, and has been increasingly true ever since, that there is no mountaineer who has a record of Himalayan climbing comparable to that of Major Bruce, which ranges

[1] Cf. *The Alpine Journal*, vol. xxiii. p. 50.

from Chitral to Sikkim. From 1889, when he first visited the mountains of Kashmir, onwards, whether on service in Chitral or Hunza, or on leave in the ranges near Abbottabad, he has never let slip an opportunity of doing as much climbing as time and circumstances permitted, and of training the Gurkhas in his regiment, hillmen born, in the art of mountaineering above the snow-line. Very properly, his zeal in this direction has been officially recognised as being what the French call "of public utility," and he has thus been enabled to carry out more extensive trips among the mountains which surround the plain of Kashmir, accompanied by his men, some of whom, through the opportunities due to his efforts, have developed into climbers of the first rank. In 1892 he bore the principal responsibility in organising Sir Martin Conway's expedition to the Karakoram, and took a very full share in its achievements, making the first passage of the Nushik La, and reaching with Conway, Matthias Zurbriggen, and two Gurkhas the summit of Pioneer Peak, 22,600 feet.

Three years later he made the preliminary arrangements for the attack on Nanga Parbat by A. F. Mummery, J. Norman Collie, and G. Hastings, which ended so deplorably in the loss of Mummery and two Gurkhas. No stronger combination of amateurs ever worked together than this party, and no Himalayan party has done so much strenuous and difficult climbing. Bruce joined them for a time, and took part in one of their most prolonged efforts.

Add to this that he has seen something of the Alps and of Alpine guides both in summer and winter, and that he possesses an unique knowledge of the languages and dialects spoken in the Himalaya, and it will be seen that his experience, both as regards actual mountaineering and in the all-important matter of organisation or *bandobast*, is unrivalled. He came to England in the summer of 1906, eager to revive Lord Curzon's scheme, and to find companions for it.

Lord Curzon's successor, Lord Minto, is himself a veteran mountaineer, and was one of the party which made the third ascent of the Schreckhorn; he was a member of the Alpine Club from 1866 to 1869, and rejoined it in 1905; his friendly interest in the project was therefore assured.

I had always looked upon those who had visited the Himalaya as the most enviable of mortals, but had never dreamed of such a piece of good fortune befalling myself; and it almost took my breath away when, in the course of a chance meeting in July 1906, Major Bruce unfolded to me his designs on Mount Everest. They were fully matured, and he already had his eye on another fellow-member of the Alpine Club, Dr. T. G. Longstaff, as a likely person to make up the party.

Dr. Longstaff has a mountaineering record little less remarkable than that of Major Bruce. He has visited most of the districts of the central and western Alps, and done much difficult climbing without guides, and in 1903 he made, with Dr. L. W. Rolleston alone, an extraordinarily brilliant and successful expedition in the Caucasus. Two years later he too accomplished a very remarkable journey in the Himalaya, of which more hereafter, and he was more than willing to return; indeed, he was already contemplating a second trip on his own account.

I had no claims to climb in such distinguished company, and the one thing which made me hesitate for a moment to grasp this golden opportunity was the fear lest I might be an encumbrance. However, I satisfied my conscience by insisting on the fact that I was middle-aged and unenterprising, and making it clear that if I could not stand high altitudes or hard work I should be prepared to accept the situation cheerfully. I felt confident that even if my worst anticipations in this respect were realised, I should still be abundantly rewarded for going.

Mount Everest lies wholly outside British India, partly in Tibet and partly in Nepal, about sixty miles west of the point where the boundaries of Nepal, Tibet, and Sikkim meet. It can be seen on a clear day at about the same distance from stations on the western border of Sikkim, which are often visited by travellers from Darjiling, and others who have penetrated farther into the mountains have had a rather nearer view of it; but it has never yet been closely approached on the Nepal side by any European. The territory of Nepal has been absolutely closed to strangers for many years, and a European can only obtain entrance to it in the capacity of a guest of the British resident at the capital, Katmandu.

For us, therefore, any idea of reaching Everest through Nepal was out of the question; our plan was to go northward through Sikkim into Tibet by the usual route, and then, turning sharply to the west, to make for its north-eastern flank. This approach involves a journey through miles of unknown and unmapped country, which may present unexpected obstacles, and is certain to be very scantily furnished with fuel, and fodder for animals, and entirely without facilities for obtaining provisions ; on the other hand, as Mount Everest has a far easier slope on the Tibetan than on the southern or Nepalese side, and as the snow-line there is much higher, being probably well above 19,000 feet, it is the one most likely to give easy access to the mountain.

Matters developed rapidly, and the financial side of the project was settled on the most satisfactory of bases, namely, that we were to bear the expenses ourselves.

Early in the autumn the Bishop of Bristol, who was at that time President of the Alpine Club, communicated full details of what was proposed to Lord Minto, and asked for his sanction and co-operation, and more especially for permission to the party to enter Tibetan territory. A telegraphic reply arrived shortly afterwards that leave for Tibet was impossible, but all facilities would be given for an attempt on Kanchenjunga.

Kanchenjunga, which, according to the most recent measurements, is credited with the height of 28,146 feet, is the monarch of the range which separates Sikkim from Nepal ; it was long supposed to be the highest mountain in the world, and though it has now had to take the third place, there is, I believe, still a possibility that when the effects of refraction are more fully understood, it may turn out to be higher than its north-western rival, K 2 (28,250 feet). Visible from Darjiling, from which it is distant only nine or ten marches, it is probably better known than any other mountain in India, and the only one, besides Everest itself, whose name is at all familiar to the outer world. Several parties of climbers have visited its neighbourhood, and more than one attempt has been made to ascend it.

But we had no mind for Kanchenjunga. To be the first people to reach Mount Everest, to set foot on its snowy sides and penetrate its glaciers, was in itself a reward sufficient to tempt any one to face many weeks of difficult travel, whether or no any serious effort could be made to reach the summit—(and I may say that none of us were sanguine enough to suppose that it was in the least degree likely that we should accomplish the latter); but in the case of Kanchenjunga the interest of exploration was wanting: it was accurately mapped; Mr. Freshfield's party had been completely round it, and its attraction centred entirely in the attempt to climb it, which would probably prove both dangerous and unsuccessful. Moreover, the neighbourhood of Kanchenjunga is singularly ill-fitted for an expedition of some months' duration, for which we were prepared. There is a notion which has considerable prevalence that the only time available for mountaineering in the Himalaya is a short period at the end of the summer after the rains have ceased, *i.e.* well on in September, which, as I experienced later, is decidedly late for climbing peaks of an elevation very much less than Kanchenjunga. The extent to which these conditions exist has perhaps been exaggerated, but they certainly hold good in a far greater degree of the mountains of Sikkim than of any other portion of the Himalaya now accessible to travellers. Therefore, if we were to be debarred from Everest, we were inclined to look for an alternative goal elsewhere.

But we had not yet quite done with Everest. Lord Minto's telegram was followed in due course by a letter, in which he expressed his own willingness to forward a visit to that mountain by every means in his power, if—and here was the crux of the situation—we could obtain the permission of the India Office at home. The matter was accordingly presented to Mr. John Morley,[1] Secretary of State for India, by Sir George Taubman-Goldie, as President of the Royal Geographical Society, and certainly no cause could have had a more able or more strenuous advocate. Though he was not successful, we cannot be too grateful for his efforts in our behalf. The correspondence on the subject is printed at length in *The Alpine Journal*,[2] and attracted some public interest at the time. Sir George Goldie, however, did not rest content with correspondence, and took the trouble to make personal representations on the subject on at least two occasions. An ingenious friend of mine expressed his good wishes on our behalf in the form of a hope that

[1] Now Lord Morley of Blackburn. [2] Vol. xxiii. p. 466.

$$\text{Mumm} + (\text{John Morley})^2 \text{ would} = \frac{\text{Mumm}}{\text{Everest}},$$

but Mr. Morley remained intractable.

His refusal was the more annoying inasmuch as it was a matter of common knowledge that, a few months earlier, the Swedish explorer, Dr. Sven Hedin, had to all intents and purposes made use of British territory as a base for an exploring expedition in Tibet of a much more extensive nature than that which we had in contemplation, though his actual entry on to Tibetan soil was made from the dominions of the Maharajah of Kashmir. Unfortunately there is no Kashmir in a suitable position at the eastern end of the Himalayan range.

The disappointment was severe, but this conclusion had been foreseen as probable, and an alternative programme had been under discussion for some time past, and, once the door was finally closed on Everest, we set about planning an expedition to an entirely different locality, where, we consoled ourselves by thinking, we should probably have more opportunity for actual climbing, and not be obliged to spend most of the time at our disposal in mere journeying to and from the scene of operations. There was also some compensation in feeling that as no great geographical discoveries were possible, we need not take the expedition too seriously, and might make pleasure its principal object. The region selected was Garhwal.

# CHAPTER II

## GEOGRAPHICAL

EVERYBODY knows that the Himalaya forms the northern boundary of India, and the majority of us at home are content to stop there, in the comfortable assurance that that knowledge suffices for all ordinary historical and political purposes, except perhaps so far as the North-West frontier is concerned. A more detailed knowledge of the range can only be acquired with a good deal of labour, and though we are told from time to time that it is over 1500 miles long, and would reach from the eastern extremity of the Alps to the western extremity of the Pyrenees, such reminders make little impression on minds accustomed to the European scale of distances. This was brought home to me last spring, when some of our Garhwal photographs were on view at the Alpine Club. There, some one who was sufficiently interested to take the trouble to come and look at them was heard to say, in a slightly aggrieved tone, that he (or she) had searched everywhere, and searched in vain, for a view of Kanchenjunga. Now the distance to Kanchenjunga from the nearest point from which any of the photographs exhibited were taken cannot be less than 600 miles.

After one has visited a place, or "got it up" with books and maps, it is curiously difficult to recall one's mental condition with regard to it at an earlier stage; but I believe that quite recently I had never heard of Garhwal or Kumaon, Almora or Kathgodam; even Naini Tal I am not sure about; Bareilly was known to me by name, because a battle was once fought there, but it was localised merely as "somewhere in India." That will give Anglo-Indians the measure of my acquaintance with Indian geography. In trying to clear the ground by the following remarks, I am assuming the reader to be in the same condition of ignorance as I was myself three years ago.

I have just joined the names of Garhwal and Kumaon; they must inevitably be dealt with together, and they furnish at once an excellent illustration of the complexities which beset one's first effort to emerge from that condition with respect to only one small fragment of the Himalaya. For there are, or have been, three Garhwals and three Kumaons: there was the old historical State of Garhwal; there are now Native or Tehri Garhwal and British Garhwal, which together cover the area of the old State; and there is the Kumaon Division, an insignificant corner of that extensive region now known as the United Provinces, which consists of two Districts, the Garhwal District or British Garhwal, and the Kumaon District, which is co-extensive with the old historical State of Kumaon. For present purposes we may disregard the old States, and Kumaon Division, and confine our attention to Garhwal, Native and British, and Kumaon District. These lie almost in the centre of the Himalayan range, Tehri Garhwal (with an area of about 4200 square miles) being the westernmost of the three. British Garhwal covers, roughly speaking, 5600 square miles, and Kumaon 6000, so that the area of the two together is about double that of Yorkshire. They contain one of the few small spaces where British India in the strict sense of the term is conterminous with Tibet. It is worth while to note this, and other similar points, because the extent of Himalayan mountain travel is largely determined, now more stringently than ever before, by the way in which the range is divided up politically. Immediately to the east of Kumaon lies the *terra clausa* of Nepal. It is about 600 miles in length, and contains more that a hundred peaks of over 21,000 feet. Of the forty-eight summits in the world which are known to exceed 25,000 feet, no less than twenty-three are within its boundaries, or, like Everest and Kanchenjunga, on its borders. As already mentioned, this country is absolutely forbidden ground to European travellers, and a mere blank so far as mountaineering exploration is concerned. Beyond Nepal is Sikkim, which is British territory, and finally at the extreme eastern end of the chain is the native State of Bhutan, inhabited by turbulent tribes and almost as completely closed to travellers as Nepal. I have already spoken of Everest and Kanchenjunga, the giants of this part of the range.

West of Garhwal the range turns slightly to the north through a number of small semi-independent States before entering Kashmir. One of these, Spiti, was the scene of some remarkable exploits by the brothers, Captain and Dr. Gerard, in 1817-21, the very first of Indian mountaineering feats; a generation later, the construction of Lord Dalhousie's Tibetan road from Simla encouraged a few mountain lovers to make high-level walking tours in that direction, some of whom went right through to Ladak and Kashmir. But the impetus died away, and these districts, though they were traversed by the ubiquitous and indefatigable Schlagintweit brothers, have on the whole been neglected by parties bent on actual mountaineering. Simla does not appear to have ever been the starting-point of a climbing expedition; indeed, the descriptions of the walking tours, to which reference has just been made, unite in representing it as a sort of Capua, with an atmosphere decidedly hostile to any such enterprise; and there are no giant peaks near at hand to exercise a counter-magnetism. Still there are plenty of mountains of a very respectable elevation (a few of them exceed 22,000 feet), and many unknown glaciers, and this intermediate region must be regarded as constituting another gap in Himalayan exploration, though very much less in extent than that formed by Nepal, and it is, of course, not in the same sense a *terra incognita*.

Beyond it we come to the vast area which forms the dominions of the Maharajah of Kashmir, and comprehends not only the western extremity of the Himalaya proper, but also a large part of the Karakoram and other great ranges to the north of the Indus, which are usually included in any survey of Himalayan exploration. Here is the most extensive, though not quite the loftiest mountain region in the world; it contains a much greater number of summits of 20,000 and 21,000 feet than Nepal, and most of the rest of those which exceed 25,000 feet; eighteen of these are on Kashmir territory or only just outside it. Though Kashmir is not under British government, the facilities for travel are very great, and far more ground has been covered by mountaineers within its boundaries than in all the rest of the Himalaya.

This rapid survey of the Himalaya from end to end is intended to suggest, amongst other things, that Garhwal and Kumaon occupy a somewhat special and isolated position both politically and in respect to mountaineering. The latter point is effectively brought out in the valuable "Sketch of the Geography and Geology of the Himalaya Mountains and Tibet," recently issued by the Indian Government, by means of a chart showing the distribution of the peaks exceeding 25,000 feet. This shows a thick cluster on the north-west, and a long line of Nepalese giants in the east, while the intermediate space is almost a blank, broken only by a single little group of three—Nanda Devi (25,645 feet) and Kamet (25,447 feet), both in British Garhwal, and the highest mountains lying wholly in British territory, and Gurla Mandhata (25,855 feet), an old acquaintance of Longstaff's, a short distance away on the other side of the Tibetan frontier. The political condition of Garhwal and Kumaon is a small historical matter, which is of some interest and may be briefly told.

It is said that the name of Garhwal is derived from the word "garh," which means a castle, and is familiar as the termination of many India place-names, and that it points back to a time when the country was under the dominion of more than fifty petty chieftains, each of whom lorded it over his dependants from the vantage-ground of a mountain stronghold. Certainly the physical features of the country lend themselves admirably to such a system, except that it is difficult to see how there could be enough dependants to go round. But this is going back to a very remote period, when a similar state of things was prevailing in the valley of the Rhine, and other mountain regions, much nearer home; in more modern times Garhwal, like Kumaon, was under the sway of a single ruler; the difficulties of access shut them off completely, save for one or two transitory in-roads, from the plains, and for centuries the two countries had no history except in so far as they were in a state of chronic warfare with each other. Late in the eighteenth century this state of affairs was put an end to for ever by a great catastrophe; the Gurkhas, then the leading race in Nepal, overran the whole of both countries, and ruled them with savage cruelty and tyranny for a generation; indeed they subjugated all the mountain territory as far west as the

Sutlej river, and it seems not inconceivable that they might have consolidated this extensive dominion, and that the closed portion of the Himalaya might have been half as large again as it now is, and the highest summit in the British Empire considerably lower. Fortunately for the mountaineering interest, they were not content to confine their activity to the hills, but commenced in-roads on the plains, and so came into collision with the British Raj. The result was the Nepalese war of 1814-15; the Gurkhas retired behind their old boundaries, western or Tehri Garhwal was restored to its native rulers, while Kumaon and British Garhwal were annexed to British India, and reduced to order by an able civilian, Commissioner G. W. Traill, who exercised a benevolent and active despotism there from 1817 to 1835.

He also forms another link between the political and climbing history of the country, for he accomplished the first recorded piece of mountaineering in it; but before proceeding to any account of his doings and those of his successors, it is necessary, at the risk of being tedious, to attempt some description of the geography and orography of the region.

Garhwal, which lies to the north and west of Kumaon, contains the principal sources of the Ganges, as well as that of its great tributary the Jumna. The latter rises in the west, then comes what is usually regarded as the main river, the Bhagirathi, and then a great affluent, the Alaknanda. The two last-named streams unite at Deoprayag, near the southern boundary of Garhwal, and the river, thenceforth known as the

Ganges, emerges into the plain a few miles farther on at the ancient and famous city of Hardwar. The basin of the Alaknanda, within which all our wanderings took place, may be said, with sufficient accuracy for present purposes, to coincide with the district of British Garhwal. It is separated from that of the Bhagirathi by a range of mountains of whose eastern peaks and glaciers we saw a good deal and photographed a little, but we hardly did more than set foot on them. The Alaknanda, again, is formed by the union of two streams known, above their junction, as the Vishnu and the Dhauli rivers.[1] They meet at Vishnuprayag near Joshimath. The range that rises between them, whose highest summit is Kamet, was the scene of the second half of our journey in Garhwal. Its northern extremity has been visited from the Tibetan side by the Schlagintweits; there is a depression in the middle of it, across which lies the easy Bhyundar pass, but for the most part it forms a tremendous barrier bristling with formidable peaks, and many of its recesses are still entirely unknown. To the east of the Dhauli-Alaknanda river lies the great mountain mass which culminates in Nanda Devi, and forms the watershed between the Dhauli and the valley of Milam in the north-eastern portion of Kumaon. The river Gori descends the Milam valley to join the Kali, along which runs the frontier line between Kumaon and Nepal, and whose waters eventually mingle with the Ganges far away to the south-east.

[1] See further on, p. 190 below, with reference to the nomenclature of these two rivers.

Of course all these mountains are regarded by geologists as forming part of two great parallel ranges running (roughly) east and west, and not north and south, the fact that they are cut through here and there by rivers being an unimportant accident. But any one writing merely as a topographer, wishful to supply a little assistance to some future editor of the Garhwal section of an "Alpine" Guide to the Himalaya, must necessarily ignore their geological continuity and group his material round the practicable routes through the country. There are only two, namely, those of Niti and Mana passes, which follow respectively the valleys of the Dhauli and Vishnu rivers, and lead across the watershed into Tibet.

The configuration of the Nanda Devi massif, which has received much more attention from travellers than the range to the west of the Dhauli river, requires a somewhat detailed examination.

On the eastern or Milam side it is fairly simple. The main axis of elevation runs north and south, parallel to the Milam valley, and rising very abruptly over it. The lateral valleys and their glaciers on this side are relatively short, sending down only insignificant tributaries to the Gori river. At its northern end the main ridge makes an abrupt turn to the east, shutting in the Milam valley on the north, and dividing it into two branches by a huge outlier which runs southward, parallel to the principal portion of the main ridge, and rises at one point to a height of 22,400 feet. In the western branch lies the great Milam glacier, by far the most considerable icefield on this side of the chain. At the head of the eastern branch the Untadhura pass (17,590 feet) provides a fairly easy passage into the upper valley of a tributary of the Dhauli called the Girthi, which thus completely encloses the Milam valley on the north.

On the west of the main chain lies an extensive group of mountains, somewhat intricate at first sight, but grouped with a certain symmetry round the Rishi river and the basin from which it flows. The southern boundary of the group is the valley of the Pindar river, a considerable tributary of the Alaknanda, which, like the Girthi, overlaps the central portion of the main ridge, and rises a little to the east of it, so that the whole massif is almost entirely embraced by the Dhauli-Alaknanda, the Girthi, and the Pindar. The valley of the last-named river is a very decisive geographical feature. Shut in closely on the south side by a range of no great elevation, it sharply divides the region of ice and snow from the civilisation of the foothills. On the other side of it the colossal outer wall of the range springs with startling rapidity to a height of 23,406 feet on Trisul, and extends eastward from that mountain nearly four miles, rarely sinking below 21,000 feet, till it articulates with the main chain. Here the main chain itself, making a south-easterly bend, continues the stupendous barrier which confronts the traveller approaching from the south, culminating in this direction in the peak of Nanda Kot (22,530 feet), near the foot of which lies the Pindari glacier. There is good going far up the Pindar valley beyond Kati, the highest village, to the Phurkea dak bungalow not far below the glacier, so that a visit can be paid to it without camping out; probably no other glacier in the Himalaya can be reached from civilised abodes so quickly and easily. The other glaciers at the foot of the great wall have, I believe, not been visited by any one except Longstaff since the time of the Great Trigonometrical Survey, forty or fifty years ago.

The Trisul range just described forms the southern bulwark of the Rishi gorge. On the north it is enclosed by another great lateral ridge of nearly equal elevation, which culminates in Dunagiri (23,184 feet), so that, ignoring details, the whole mass may be regarded as a reversed and inverted Ⅎ enclosed in a rude triangle, of which the Pindar river is the base, the Rishi valley being formed by the two horizontal spokes of the Ⅎ. The gorge of the Rishi river is an extraordinary one, but the most singular feature of the region yet remains to be mentioned. Right across, from the Dunagiri ridge to the Trisul ridge, extends a fourth massive block of mountain, running north and south, parallel to the central portion of the main chain, and enclosing a sort of parallelogram, about seven miles by five, the only break in which is the narrow and precipitous cleft through which the Rishi has carved its way out. Into and across this basin projects Nanda Devi itself, its north-western arête descending almost to the entrance of the chasm.

The remarkable situation of Nanda Devi arrests the attention directly one casts an eye over the map, and the first thing which attracted me when I began to study the geography of the district was the prospect of setting foot on and exploring the icy sea by which it appears to be surrounded.

This icy sea is not quite so continuous a mass of glacier as the map represents it to be, and probably some of its other details may require to be modified; but the indications given that the approach to Nanda Devi is extremely well guarded, are, in the main, correct.

I may as well state at this point that the map here referred to is the one usually known as the G.T.S. map, produced by the labours of the Great Trigonometrical Survey, which I have just mentioned. The scale is a mile to an inch, but a smaller and very handy edition (four miles to an inch) is also obtainable. The discovery of errors in it was to us a source of excitement and pleasure which I cannot in the least explain, but which I believe every one will understand who has travelled in regions which are imperfectly known. But we felt nothing but admiration for the way in which the surveyors in Garhwal did their work. Considering the means at their disposal and the immense difficulties of the country, one can only wonder that they attained so high a degree of completeness and accuracy.

The first recorded mountaineering exploit in the neighbourhood of Nanda Devi was the crossing by Commissioner Traill of a pass at the head of the Pindari glacier leading into the Milam valley, about the year 1830. This pass has been known by his name ever since. A remark of Adolph Schlagintweit's suggests, probably correctly, that his object was not mountain exploration, but that he was seeking for a short-cut to Milam, which would be useful for commercial purposes.

In 1855 he was followed by Adolph Schlagintweit, who learned that Traill had suffered severely from snow-blindness, and was told by the natives that he had only recovered after making a substantial offering to the temple of Nanda Devi at Almora: the facts from which this legend originated were that Traill, soon after his return, had had to settle a dispute between the Brahmins of this temple and the British Government, with regard to the property in some plots of land, and decided the case in favour of the temple, a piece of uprightness which was unintelligible to native ideas without at least the co-operation of other grounds than that of justice.

Schlagintweit himself had to promise not only additional pay, but a rich offering to Nanda Devi in order to persuade thirty of the strongest people in the Dhanpur district to go with him. He took the further precaution of providing each of them with a piece of green gauze as a protection against the glare. An old man, the sole survivor of the hundred people who had accompanied Traill, acted as guide.

On the night of May 30 the party slept in the open at a height of 14,180 feet, and started at 1.30 A.M. It was not practicable to follow the main valley, and they had to go up a side glacier, and cross from it on to the upper névé of the Pindari glacier over a col (17,770 feet, the highest point attained), which he reached at eight o'clock. Here he commenced to make observations, but was disagreeably interrupted by three of his hardiest men in rapid succession being seized with epileptic fits. They threw themselves on the snow, rolled their eyes, struck about with hands and feet, and gave every indication of being out of their senses. A cry rose up that Nanda Devi had entered into them, and Adolph, fearful lest the seizure might spread further, took aside two Brahmins whom he had with him, and after pointing out that he had given Nanda Devi all that they had demanded, and that this unpleasant scene was only the result of their own folly in calling on Nanda Devi at every difficult place on the way up, ordered them, under threats of severe punishment at Almora, to put a stop to it at once. This they achieved, partly by prayers, and partly by putting snow on the heads of the sufferers, the latter remedy being in Adolph's opinion the more effective of the two. Descending by the "Loan" (Lwanl) glacier, he camped under a big overhanging rock at Narspan Patti, and next day joined his brother Robert at Milam. Together they ascended the Pagu horn and explored the great Milam glacier, then leaving the Milam valley by the Untadhura route, crossed another pass from the upper basin of the Girthi into Tibet.

Some weeks later they made their memorable ascent to 22,239 feet on "Ibi Gamin" (which has been universally assumed to be identical with Kamet) from the Tibetan side, and reached the Mana pass from the north. They were thus altogether outside the area of our journeyings, except that their route coincided with ours along the Mana pass road.

In 1861 Traill's pass was again traversed by Colonel Edmund Smyth, a climber who deserves honourable mention in any sketch of mountaineering in Garhwal.

He is the still surviving brother of the Rev. Christopher Smyth and the Rev. J. Grenville Smyth, who were very prominent members of the Alpine brotherhood in its very earliest stages, and are now best remembered as having belonged to the first party which reached the highest summit of Monte Rosa, and to the enterprising band who made the famous guideless ascent of Mont Blanc from St. Gervais, organised by Charles Hudson and E. S. Kennedy. These events took place in 1855, but already in the memorable year 1854 they had ascended the Strahlhorn, the first of the great peaks round Zermatt to be climbed, with the exception of the Breithorn, and had reached the Ost Spitze of Monte Rosa; and in both these expeditions Colonel Smyth took part. He was then about thirty years of age, and subsequently spent many years in Garhwal as Inspector of the Educational Department.

In the course of official and shooting trips he wandered far and wide amongst the mountains, and earned the reputation among the natives of being able to climb "where birds could not fly." No doubt his Alpine experience stood him in good stead. He has crossed at least two other glacier passes—the Bhyundar pass, where we followed him in 1907, and the Ralam pass. He has not written of his doings himself, but fortunately some accounts of them from his own mouth have been preserved by General Macintyre in his charming book, *The Hindu Koh*; and one of his most interesting journeys, in the course of which he reached the base of Gurla Mandata, is graphically described by Mr. T. W. Webber in *The Forests of Upper India.*

In 1883 Mr. T. S. Kennedy, a well-known Alpine climber, visited the Milam valley with Johann Jaun, but was unable to attempt any high climbing, and devoted himself to sport instead. The only memorial of his journey is a panoramic view of the mountains at the head of the Lwanl valley, which was recently presented by Mr. Edward Whymper to the Alpine Club, on whose walls it now hangs.

More interest attaches to the journey of Dr. Kurt Boeckh in 1893. He had already been in Sikkim, and did not start from Almora till July 1, when the rains were in full swing. He visited the Pindari glacier, and was informed by the native herdsmen that no white man had been there since the surveyors, except one English sportsman, who had been attacked by a bear on the glacier, and killed. The natives also said that the glacier had retreated so much, and was so broken, that the route to Traill's pass was no longer practicable. He did not attempt to test the truth of this statement, and, after spending a fortnight of unceasing rain in the Phurkea dak bungalow, proceeded by a rough cross-country route to the Gori valley, and up it to Milam.

From Milam he visited the Milam glacier, and ascended a point which he calls Panschakuri, on the ridge which separates it from the main valley of the Gori. He then went up the "Mongschapu" glacier, hoping to discover a practicable pass across the main chain to the north of Nanda Devi, but his coolies, when they realised what his plans were, refused to accompany him. Had the attempt been made, it must have ended in defeat or disaster. Having had a view, though only a distant and imperfect one, of the other side of the chain at this point, I think that, supposing they had been able to reach the summit ridge, they might have got down into the great basin surrounding Nanda Devi, which I have already attempted to describe: but I do not believe that a party consisting mainly of loaded coolies would have ever got out of it again alive, except by the way that they came.

Dr. Boeckh, however, was determined, come what might, not to retrace his steps, so he sent most of his baggage back to Almora and Naini Tal, and with some difficulty persuaded five coolies to cross the Untadhura pass with him, and try the descent of the Girthi valley.

They left Milam on September 8, and after encountering formidable difficulties in the precipitous gorges of the Girthi and Uja Tirche rivers, arrived safely at Malari in the valley of the Dhauli on or about the 17th. This was a really remarkable performance. I do not know of any other European having effected the passage, though it was certainly known to the natives, and may possibly have been traversed by sportsmen. From Malari, Dr. Boeckh returned by the Niti pass road to Joshimath. As in the case of the Schlagintweits, his path coincided with ours only for a short distance along a main valley route.

Some years later Dr. Boeckh described his journey at great length in his *Indische Gletscherfahrten;*

*Reisen und Erlebnisse im Himalaya*; and his detailed day-to-day narrative will repay perusal by any one who meditates undertaking a similar one, without having had some previous experience of Indian travel, inasmuch as it gives an accurate and vivid picture of the troubles and worries that inevitably beset a traveller unfamiliar with the country and language, troubles and worries of which, thanks to the skilled leadership enjoyed by our party, I remained in an ignorance which was entirely blissful. The laconic utterances, too, of his Tyrolese guide, Hans Kerer of Kals, are delightful, and I cannot resist the temptation to reproduce one specimen of them.

They had arrived at Milam with their stock of silver coin nearly exhausted, and found, to their consternation, that the inhabitants were unable to change the gold pieces on which they relied. There was nothing for it but to send a runner with them to Almora, to get them changed there, and to meet them with a fresh supply of rupees later on at Joshimath.

Parting with the money to a native was bad enough —one can picture the anguish of a guide at being forced to such a course,—but this was not all: the contemplated recipient of the money was the Rev. Mr. O. of Almora, and Kerer comments: "Der englische Missionar hat doch für Frau und Kinder zu sorgen! Du hättest das Geld besser an den Jesuitenpater in Almora geschickt." One is glad to know that the rupees came safely to hand at Joshimath; and indeed, so far as my own observation went, I should say that these poor mountain folk are a very honest lot.

Dr. Boeckh, like all the other explorers hitherto mentioned of the Nanda Devi massif, confined his attention to the eastern and southern sides. But ten years earlier, in the same year as that of Mr. Kennedy's visit, it had been subjected to a far more formidable attack, when Mr. W. W. Graham, with Emil Boss and Ulrich Kaufmann, approached it for the first time from the west.

Graham's achievements in the Himalaya in 1883 have had a very remarkable history. His account of them was, at the time, the subject of a warm and quite voluminous controversy, and still possesses a curious power of provoking partisanship. But the debate raged exclusively round his later doings in Sikkim, particularly his alleged ascent of the second summit, only 30 or 40 feet lower than the highest point (24,015 feet) of Kabru, the only mountain exceeding 24,000 feet which has hitherto been tried with any degree of success.

That portion of his narrative which deals with Garhwal has never been subjected to a detailed examination. I shall have to treat of it at some length, but will reserve all comment till we arrive on the scene of action ourselves. For the present, it is enough to say that after trying without success to follow the course of the Rishi river from its mouth, he made a determined attempt to scale Dunagiri from the west, and then entered the Rishi valley by the route afterwards taken by us: he was unable to force the passage of the Rishi cleft into the Nanda Devi basin, but assailed two other peaks, and reached the summit of one of them. What is important at this stage is, that his description so stirred Longstaff's imagination that when the opportunity of visiting the Himalaya came to him in 1905, he determined to follow in Graham's footsteps. "My intention was," he wrote in *The Alpine Journal*, "to try Trisul (23,406 feet) from the south—it is only 60 miles from Naini Tal—and then march up into Garhwal, and, in imitation of Graham, attempt some peaks of the Nanda Devi group from the west. Failing this, there was Ibi Gamin (Kamet) and its attendant peaks to the northward, where I hoped the effects of the monsoon would be less marked than in the southern ranges. I put this upon record because, should I ever go there again, that is the plan I should follow." Surely this was a direct challenge to Providence to thwart him, but Longstaff is one of those people on whom Providence smiles. He was diverted from his plans, on his arrival at Almora, by an invitation from Mr. C. A. Sherring, the Deputy Commissioner, to accompany him in a tour up the Milam valley, which ultimately developed into a tour in Tibet. He spent about three weeks in the Milam valley, visiting one after another all the lateral valleys which descend from Nanda Devi and Nanda Kot, and making two good passes over their dividing ridges. He also reached the height of about 21,000 feet on Nanda Kot, and about 20,000 feet on the eastern peak of Nanda Devi.

In the course of their attempt on the latter peak the party camped just to the south of it, on the summit ridge of the main chain. They were the first and only people to reach it at any point between Traill's pass and the Untadhura pass, and the first to look down on to the glaciers of the Nanda Devi basin, a descent to which Longstaff considered to be practicable. Moreover, during their ascent on the following day they had a good view of the north-eastern and eastern sides of Trisul, and came to the conclusion that there was a fairly easy way to the summit up the north-eastern snow-slopes.

At the end of June they joined Mr. Sherring and went up the valley of the Kali into Tibet, where they spent a thrilling week in an attempt on Gurla Mandhata, and a month later, crossing the Shel Shel and Chor Hoti passes, descended into the valley of the Dhauli just below Niti village.

During this part of their journey Longstaff had many distant views of the upper part of Kamet, and what he saw led him to think that it might be attacked with a good prospect of success, and also confirmed him in the hope that the rains would not, so far north, be a serious obstacle to mountaineering.

He then descended the Niti pass road, and, making his way to the Pindar valley, visited two of the glaciers at the foot of the southern face of Trisul early in October. There he satisfied himself that Trisul was impracticable from the southern side, and that by far the most promising route to its summit was the one which he had inspected in the previous June.

So it came about that when, in the following year, our prospects of getting to Everest became doubtful, Longstaff was not only prepared with a ready-made programme, but had also a considerable stock of first-hand knowledge and experience bearing directly on the practicability of its different items. There was no rival plan in the field; Bruce was very ready for a visit to a district of which he had, as yet, had only distant views, and to me it was the Himalaya, and I wanted no more.

## CHAPTER III

### LONDON TO ALMORA

On matters of equipment, etc., I have not much to say, though many hours were very enjoyably spent in discussing them. I had had a very limited experience of camp life, and was in the hands of two experts, and well satisfied to leave all details to them; besides which I could never remember from one meeting to another how many pounds went to a *maund* and how many to a *seer*.

Bruce left England in February, and the supply of provisions and stores was left in his very competent hands, to be dealt with in India. Our contribution in this department consisted of two primus stoves and half a dozen large thermos bottles, which were of great service. We treated ourselves handsomely in the matter of tents, taking out from England five Whymper tents and five Mummery tents, while a large mess-tent, sent by Bruce, met us a fortnight or so after we started. Thus, when on ordinary march, we had a Whymper tent apiece, except the brothers Brocherel, who invariably shared one between them. Two persons can get on very well in a Whymper tent for a time, but it would become irksome if this state of things went on continuously for a long period. Besides, it is essential to have plenty of elbow-room in the matter of tents, since circumstances may easily arise when tents may be wanted in two or more different places at once, and when some may be unavoidably out of use. At one time, as will be seen, we had three, if not four establishments running at the same time, as well as an unoccupied base-camp.

We also brought some camp-beds out with us, but never used them. This was rather a shock to me at first, as I had been taught in Africa to regard a bedstead as being in the first rank of necessaries. But there is not the same danger in the Himalaya from sleeping on the ground, and I am bound to say that we got on very well without them. But I owed much to the loan of a circular air-cushion belonging to Longstaff.

Down sleeping-bags were provided for the whole party. They are expensive, but this is the only thing that can be urged against them; they are very light, pack into a very small space, and their efficiency as a protection against cold is amazing. Though I am at least as sensitive to cold as the average, I was nearly always comfortably warm at night, and never suffered severely.

I took out, as my special contribution to our outfit, some oxygen generators, or pneumatogen cartridges, manufactured by Siebe, Gorman and Co., Limited, of Westminster Bridge Road. They are intended to be employed in mines where the air is foul, but I thought they might be useful at great heights. However, I never could get any of the others to take much interest in them, and no really good opportunity offered itself of testing their efficiency.

The only other articles of equipment of which special mention need be made, were our valises, which were made of Willesden canvas on a pattern devised by Bruce, and patented by him under the designation of "the Lyte Wate," a name which draws attention to one of their principal merits. The other conspicuous feature in their construction is that there is nothing rigid or unyielding or sharply angular about them, so that they are very well adapted for carrying in places where loads are borne on the back and not on the head.

Longstaff was rather in favour of a guideless expedition, but he was in a minority, and did not press the point. Once it was decided to bring guides, there was no hesitation as to who they should be; the brothers Alexis and Henri Brocherel, of Courmayeur, had accompanied Longstaff on his previous journey, and shown very great ability, endurance, and resourcefulness in emergencies; they were chosen naturally and inevitably. I suggested the addition of Moritz Inderbinen, of Zermatt, with whom I had climbed, on and off, for more than twenty years, and who had accompanied Mr. Freshfield and me to the foot of Ruwenzori two years before. This was a piece of personal luxury; I hankered after the presence of some one who would be a stand-by in case I could not do as much as the others; but they might reasonably have objected that he was unnecessary, and that his presence would make the party unwieldy. However, they very good-naturedly refrained from raising that point; it was even considered that an extra man might be useful in the event of any temporary splitting up of the party on two simultaneous expeditions; a very possible contingency, though it did not actually occur. I should have been very much less happy than I was if he had not come.

It had from the first been contemplated that Bruce should if possible obtain leave for some of his Gurkhas to accompany us, partly with a view to their own education, partly because they were likely to be useful in numerous ways, whether European guides accompanied us or not. And, last but by no means least, he was to bring his own cook with him.

Longstaff and I left London on April 4, and next morning joined Inderbinen and the Brocherels at Marseilles. Neither Inderbinen nor I had met the Brocherels before, and I was a trifle anxious as to how they would hit it off together; there might be a certain element of international jealousy and mistrust in their relations; it was a standing matter of chaff against Inderbinen when we were in Africa that Zermatt was a sort of Arcadia, where, if anything ever did go wrong, the Italians were sure to be at the bottom of it. But an *entente cordiale* was established at once, and they remained the best of friends throughout. The Brocherels' languages are Italian and French, Inderbinen's German and English, but they never seemed to have any difficulty in carrying on a conversation.

Later on, Inderbinen used to give English lessons on off-days in camp.

The voyage out was very pleasant, and quite uneventful. Of course there were endless talks about what we were going to do, but I can only recall one fragment which is worth reporting. My prevailing mood was very optimistic; in my more sanguine moods I used to picture us bringing back the top of Nanda Devi to grace the Alpine Club Jubilee, and one day I asked Longstaff, "How many big peaks do you think we shall manage? Four or five?" I was much disconcerted when he answered soberly, "I shall be very well satisfied if we get up one."

A letter from Bruce was awaiting us at Aden saying that he would have everything ready for a start by the time we got to Almora, and urging us to come through with all possible speed: and a telegram of like tenor met us on our arrival in India on Friday, April 19: so we went on by train the same evening, having seen nothing of Bombay but some very European-looking streets, the Law Courts, and the Army and Navy stores.

Very early on Sunday morning we left the main line at Bareilly, and got into the little narrow-gauge railway that leads to the edge of the foothills: the atmosphere was extraordinarily clear, and we had some wonderful glimpses of a snowy range towering above them, probably Trisul and the ridge to the east of it, about a hundred miles away: unluckily the train was travelling point-blank in that direction, and it was only for a few minutes that one had a chance of seeing it.

There must have been a marvellous view that morning from Bareilly, if there was any one there to care for such things.

The terminus, Kathgodam, known to the British soldier as "Pussy be blowed," is interesting only on account of its situation on the edge of the hills. It is very well known to residents in India as the end of the railway route to Naini Tal, the principal hill station of the United Provinces, fifteen miles away, which can be reached in about three hours; there is a good carriage road almost the whole way.

Naini Tal had been originally fixed upon for rendezvous with Bruce; there we were to deposit our heavy trunks and superfluous garments, etc., and there I had hoped to have a breathing-space of one clear day, in which to rearrange the contents of my baggage. But Bruce's message was urgent, and this necessary and complicated process had to be got through in about two hours in the Kathgodam waiting-room. However, it was accomplished somehow, and no serious blunders were made. Meanwhile Longstaff was taking charge of the situation outside in a masterful manner, and haranguing a score or so of coolies volubly, and, to all-seeming, intelligibly, in Hindustani. In all the rush and hurry of the last few days there had been nothing unfamiliar, nothing to bring home to one that Europe had been left far behind; but this little scene left no doubt about it. The abandoned articles were left to go to Naini Tal by mail-cart, and about mid-day we started to ride up to our first stage, the little lake of Bimthal, where I spent my first night in a dak bungalow, without bedding or a change of clothes, for the coolies thought fit to stop and spend the night somewhere on the road, and did not put in an appearance till next morning—another reminder that we were really "east of Suez."

In what seemed but a few minutes after leaving Kathgodam a sombre forest-clad gorge swallowed us; all sight of the plains vanished, and we were in a new world, a world of lofty hills on which, if they were dumped down anywhere in Europe, the name of "mountains" would be bestowed, and epithets like "magnificent" would be freely lavished. Here they are just "the foothills." It is an extremely complicated region, a labyrinth of deep valleys turning and twisting in every direction, whose intricacies once formed a fairly effectual barrier between the more open country beyond and the greater world of India. Now it is traversed by numerous tracks, which, though often exceedingly steep, are rideable. The late Mr. Alfred Williams, who crowned a long career as a mountain artist by a courageous and successful frontal attack on the Himalaya at the age of seventy, used to say that these hills were ugly. Perhaps they are not, in the original and narrow sense of the word, picturesque; they have not much outline, and may not group themselves naturally into a "composition," but the road through them, now crawling up their great sides, clad from base to crest with splendid forest, now following the curves of a spacious hollow filled with oak and rhododendron, or topping some tall ridge from which one gets a surprise glimpse of the blue expanse of the plains, is brimful of interest for an unsophisticated newcomer. On the northern slope of this mountainous belt stands the last of the dak bungalows before Almora is reached. It is called Peora, and enjoys what I do not hesitate to say is one of the finest distant mountain views in the world. The country immediately in front of it is broken up by numerous deep-cut river channels into an intricate system of ridges, but the summits of these are, comparatively speaking, level, and the general effect on the eye is that of a vast plateau, seamed here and there with narrow ravines, extending to the Pindar watershed. Beyond this foreground, in the centre of the panorama, rises the great southern wall of the Nanda Devi-Trisul massif, extending eastward from Trisul to Nanda Kot, with the two summits of Nanda Devi rising beyond and between them, and continued to the west in the graceful outline of Nanda Ghunti.

To the east of Nanda Kot is a very beautiful group of sharp peaks, the Panch Chuli or Five Fires, between the Gori and Kali rivers, and beyond these again were visible some of the unknown giants of Nepal. Longstaff had thoughtfully so arranged our itinerary that we should spend a night at Peora in order that I might have as good a chance as possible of getting this view. It was certainly well worth it.

Only the recesses of an invisible ravine, and a short half-day's march, now separated us from the Almora ridge, where Bruce was waiting, with everything in readiness, eager to be off. Its buildings were plainly visible, and the commanding position, which has made it the centre of Kumaon politics from time immemorial, was obvious at a glance.

Almora was formally constituted the capital of Kumaon more than three centuries ago, and has remained so ever since. The decisive event in the war with the Gurkhas, to which reference has already been made, was its capture by the British under Colonel Hutchinson in April 1815. The result of the negotiations which followed was that the Gurkhas evacuated all their recent conquests, and retired over the Kali river, with their arms and baggage, the transport and supplies being provided by the British.

"It seems evident, however, from the details which have been published, that the contest has been with a bold and adventurous foe, with whom the establishment of a lasting pacification is, perhaps, more to be desired than expected."

Such was the impression made at home at the time, and in view of what we have learned since of the fighting qualities of the Gurkhas, it is not a surprising one.

But the forecast has been happily and very completely falsified. Our relations with Nepal are indeed irritating to would-be travellers, who find themselves shut out of a large and seductive section of the mountains of India; but the Government considers a scrupulous respect for the policy of exclusion dear to the Nepalese a cheap price to pay for the invaluable privilege of free access to their territory as a recruiting ground. That Almora should become the administrative centre of Kumaon was natural, but it is certainly a curious outcome of the whirligig of time that it is now the headquarters of the 3rd Gurkha Rifles.

It has a charm of its own, with its bungalows scattered over the wooded slopes on tiny terraces, no two of which are of the same elevation, its spacious outlook, and noble view of the snows. Parts of the old fortress still remain, a link with the obliterated past, and the native town, lying along the bare spine of the ridge, appeared supremely picturesque to my unaccustomed eyes. A little while only, and one would take as much interest in it as a Londoner does in the Tower. As a permanent residence Almora has the defects of its situation, and is an extremely awkward place to get away from. The orthodox way, for example, of going to the golf-links—of course there are golf-links—is to get on a bicycle, and "coast" down for three or four miles (with a good chance of meeting nervous cows round any of the numerous corners); then you ride or drive back and a "boy" wheels up the bicycle.

But my recollections of Almora belong mostly to the return journey, when I spent several days there, and had an interesting experience of one of the various phases of Anglo-Indian life, and of its unique product, Anglo-Indian hospitality.

Our stay on the way out was brief, and fully occupied. We arrived at mid-day on April 24—twenty days from London—and were allowed a halt of only one day. Bruce was staying with Captain Shuttleworth, and there we found him surrounded by stores and parcels, which filled the bedroom and overflowed into the verandah, and by some of his Gurkhas, who were camping in the compound close by.

I take this opportunity of saying that Captain Shuttleworth had been taking infinite trouble to assist Bruce in his preparations, and that the whole party is deeply indebted to him. He and Mr. Jackson, who shared his bungalow, spared no pains to make us all comfortable during our stay, and kindly took charge of our remaining civilised garments, which we were now shedding. The evening of our arrival was the regimental guest night, so that we also had a pleasant opportunity of making the acquaintance of most of the other officers of the regiment; moreover, we met Mr. Davis, a resident in Kumaon, whose ardour for shikar had led him into the depths of the Rishi valley, and from whom we obtained some useful topographical information about that mysterious place.

For the rest hurry and bustle prevailed, Bruce in the centre of the stage carrying on interviews with divers personages in strange languages, and sending messengers hither and thither. It was absorbingly interesting if one had had more time to take it in.

There was one abiding impression; here, once for all, I realised the Gurkha. Later association with him developed the picture, but the main outline did not change. What struck me at once, and gave the clue to their character as a race, and the attraction that they possess for Englishmen, was the footing they were on with Bruce. It also struck another observer, Alexis Brocherel. Now Alexis is a bit of a philosopher, much interested in the relations between different kinds of human beings, and never quite happy till he has analysed his impressions, and put them into shape; I always enjoyed a talk with him. He has served, too, in the Italian army as a sergeant in a mountain battery, and so had a standard of comparison to start from. He took an early opportunity of explaining his views on the subject. I wish I could give them in his own words, but the gist of them was that he had known many good officers, for whom the men felt affection and admiration; but that an officer should be on such terms of familiar good-fellowship with his men, and that the elements of respect and discipline should not be in the least degree impaired, was to him novel, and, if he had not seen it, incredible.

I think that what interested Alexis most was the part that Bruce's own personality played in all this, and, of course, it did play a large part; but the Gurkha character was at least an equally essential factor.

Casting about for an analogy that would be illuminating to people at home, I have said, more than once, that they were like schoolboys spending a holiday with a very popular master; and though it would be impossible to imagine any one less pedagogic than Bruce, I cannot find a better. Throughout the journey they reminded one in a hundred ways of schoolboys out for a holiday. They all of them looked absurdly young. They took a boyish delight in throwing stones at any mark, animate or inanimate, that offered itself, and all, I may add, were natural good shots. One or two of them further resembled schoolboys in the possession of a most engaging love of chaff and practical jokes, and no trait could show more decidedly the gulf between them and all other native races. And, withal, they were ready, at a moment's notice, to spring to attention, so to speak, and become alert, obedient, prepared to go anywhere and do anything. I have often been asked whether they are not like the Japanese; my notions of the Japanese are derived entirely from books, but I should say that the resemblance is superficial, except that both races are small, neatly made, supple, tough and muscular. Japanese urbanity and cheerfulness seems to strike close observers as being deliberate, the expression of a principle; the Gurkha's light-heartedness is spontaneous, and his good manners perfectly simple and natural. Both are warlike and brave, but I cannot imagine a Gurkha making war in a spirit of self-immolation, and courting death on the field of glory; he would regard it, rather, as the most supremely interesting of games, in which the stakes are his life or the enemy's, and getting killed unnecessarily would, in his eyes, be simply playing the game badly.

It is impossible to overstate our debt of gratitude to the authorities, and especially Colonel Kemball, the commanding officer of the 5th Gurkhas, for giving leave to so large a number of men to accompany our party. Not only were they of incalculable service, in great things and small, throughout the whole journey, but they added vastly to that which is the real though unacknowledged object of all such journeys—

> The fun, and the joy of eventful living.

# CHAPTER IV

## ALMORA TO THE DHAULI VALLEY

We started from Almora on April 26 on foot; a pony was to have been provided for me, as I was considered to be unwell (sickening for fever; so it was put later), but it failed to appear, and after an hour or two I was very glad that it had not. The ridge runs on for some miles to the foot of the hill of Bhinsar, on which Mr. Williams lived for some weeks in 1902; the summit must command an even finer view of the Trisul ridge than that from Peora. We had intended to walk over it, and I wish we had, but there was a failure of the water supply at the place where the roads diverge, and going on would have meant tiffin without anything to drink—an obstacle which seemed overwhelmingly cogent at the time.

The route for the next forty-eight hours lay through rich alluvial valleys, broad and level, cultivated and populous, one of the rare tracts in Kumaon of its kind. Comfortable dak bungalows were still available at night, and the second and third day's journeys were very pleasantly broken by tiffin with the owners of two of the few tea plantations which still remain in the country. Our hosts on the first occasion were Captain Troupe of Kausani and his brother, the former a veteran of the mutiny, who had taken part in the

siege and storming of Delhi almost exactly fifty years before.

On the 28th we came, about mid-day, to the bungalow of Mr. and Mrs. Nash at Gwaldam, the last outpost of white civilisation, charmingly situated on a depression in the chain of hills that overlooks the Pindar river. Wooded slopes rose on either hand, and behind us, over wooded slopes that we had just ascended, was the spacious prospect of the foothills, to which we were now bidding farewell. But our interest was absorbed in what lay in front, beyond the Pindar; for Trisul was now in sight, no longer seen as part of a ridge, but a single summit, its triple crest gleaming against the sky.

At Gwaldam we were joined by a very important personage, the general manager and organiser of the coolies, Lachman by name, who remained with us till the end of July, and whose efficient performance of his duties added greatly to our comfort. He was sent by Mr. V. A. Stowell, the Deputy Commissioner of Garhwal, to whom our best thanks are due for providing us with so capable and business-like a person.

In order to make clear our proceedings of the succeeding week, it is necessary to explain that the Pindar and the Dhauli-Alaknanda meet about thirty-three miles to the west of Trisul; three considerable ridges ramifying from Trisul occupy the intervening tract of country, which lies almost wholly below the snow-line, and contains a large number of scattered villages. We proposed to make a more or less high-level route across it, reaching the Dhauli valley by the Kuari pass, near the mouth of the Rishi gorge, and it was part of Longstaff's original plan to devote some days to exploring two glens at the head of the first of the intervening valleys, which run right up to the base of Trisul, and contain two glaciers about which very little is known.

The highest portion of the first of the three ridges, above mentioned, was now immediately in front of us, a long uncouth mass, with the uncouth name of Dhunga Bukhtial. It was pretty thickly covered with snow, and had attracted my attention at Peora, where I had asked Longstaff if it were a genuine snow mountain, or not. He pronounced it an impostor, and we now obtained the additional information that it would by this time be almost free from snow in most years. This, I think, was the first intimation we

received that the season was an unusually late one.

Descending through the terraced tea plantations we entered Garhwal, crossed the river by a fine suspension bridge, and pitched camp at Dewal, a mile or two farther up. Here we said good-bye to houses, beds, table-cloths, and a good many other things for three months.

The way lay over a depression between Dhunga Bukhtial and Trisul, at the head of the river Wan, and two short marches brought us to the upper level of the valley where Wan village lies, within easy distance of the pass. It would have been easy to push on to Kanol, a village just on the other side; but we wished to ascend a point to the right of the pass, marked 11,949 on the G.T.S. map, which gave promise of a view, also to enjoy an afternoon at Wan, a place with a reputation.

And indeed the grassy plateau, a few hundred feet above the river, surrounded by splendid clumps of surai pines, formed an ideal camping-ground. We found the tents pitched, and showing up brightly against the trees; the Gurkhas had erected a smart booth of bamboos, and festooned it with rhododendrons. It made a pretty picture, one of those which live in the memory, and recalled to me a remark made just before I left England by a former Himalayan traveller: "It isn't the climbing that you'll enjoy in the Himalaya; *that* is a beastly grind; it's the camps under the deodars."

Next morning, passing traces of the recent presence of wild pig, and the corpses of numerous locusts which had been swept up by the wind and dropped there, frozen, we reached the pass (10,000 feet) in about an hour and a quarter, and there touched snow for the first time. From our little peak there was a magnificent view—well worth an extra day—of Nanda

WAN CAMP

Ghunti, and the west face of Trisul. Inderbinen looked longingly at the latter; why weren't we going to try it? it was no steeper than the Zinal side of the Gabelhorn, he murmured; but the suggestion fell flat. He was probably right as regards the steepness; what he had not thought about was that the Zinal side of

the Gabelhorn was not a suitable place to spend several successive nights on.

We dropped down to Kanol in about an hour, discovering on the way that there is nothing like a bamboo stem hidden under snow or leaves for putting you neatly and instantaneously on your back.

A terrific storm burst on us at about six o'clock, an unusually late hour; it passed over, but recommenced in the night with even greater violence. I was drowsily aware once of some one hammering at the pegs of my tent, and noticed that the roof was rather slack, so I blessed the Gurkhas and slumbered again. Next morning I was hailed by Bruce with: "Well, you slept well last night."—"Did I? Well, I think I did, thanks."—"Yes, your tent came down on top of you, and you never noticed it: I put it up again." I felt all the gratitude the occasion called for; I only hope I expressed it adequately.

Bruce had been deeply impressed by the amount of snow on and around the little peak we had just ascended, and now pronounced so emphatically against attempting any exploration of the head of the Sutol glens in their present condition, that it was agreed to abandon that project, or postpone it till our return, and to go straight on at once to the Rishi valley. Bruce has had some terrific experiences of avalanches in the Karakoram and the neighbourhood of Nanga Parbat, and rightly leaned to the side of over-caution, if indeed possible to be over-cautious on such a matter. I think, however, it may safely be said that avalanches do not occur in Garhwal on the same appalling and incalculable scale as in those regions; they are, broadly speaking, Alpine in character.

The coolies, too, had an eye on the snow; when the change of plans was made known to them, they displayed considerable reluctance to face the Kuari pass, and demanded to be taken down the river to its junction with the Alaknanda, and then up the main road—a dull round of several days,—but their objections were overruled.

The two valleys which now lay between us and the

Kuari pass are remarkably similar in general character, so far as our acquaintance with them extended. A typical section of either of them would resemble, not a V but a Y, the stem representing the narrow precipitous gorge at the bottom through which the river cleaves its way. They are not, however, symmetrical, the southern slopes being much more uniform, those on the northern side broken by plateaux elevated far above the stream. Another very marked feature, which was reproduced in varying degrees in all valleys running east and west in which forest existed, was that the southern slopes were far more thickly wooded than the northern ones. This, I suppose, is in some way due to the larger amount of sun which falls on the former; it occurs in places where it cannot be accounted for by human agency, though that may sometimes contribute to it. The natural result in the country now before us was that the principal track, and the great majority of the villages and hamlets, lay along the northern side of the valleys, and the bridges were found high up, above the gorges.

We descended from Kanol to the Nandakganga just below the junction of its two branches, and had a glorious view of Trisul swathed in morning mists at the head of the main glen; a long pull up-hill, and a hot trudge down the valley, high above the now invisible river, brought us to Ramni village. Here we found awaiting us the rest of the Gurkhas, and a large quantity of stores. A hundred pounds of tea, the produce of the Troupes' garden at Kausani, had gone astray, and its whereabouts remained a mystery for some time afterwards, but otherwise all was well, and a sufficient number of additional coolies had been collected. This was no small matter, as there was a formidable number of loads to be carried, and the augmented caravan, during the next three days, when it was probably at its maximum, amounted to about one hundred and fifty.

The new contingent was under the command of Jemmadar Kharbir Thapa, the senior in age and rank of the Gurkhas, and one of the most important members of our party. He is a regular Indian Ulysses, has travelled as far afield as Wales, and enjoyed an extensive and varied experience both of climbing and of fighting. He took part in most of Bruce's expeditions in Khagan and Kashmir, and accompanied him to the Karakoram in 1892, though he was on the sick-list at the time of the ascent of Pioneer Peak. Two years later he saw "the Alps from End to End," under Sir Martin Conway's leadership. As a mountaineer he is in the very first rank. He possesses all the attractive qualities of the other Gurkhas except their appearance of extreme youthfulness: his weather-beaten face gave no clue to his age; I should have guessed that he was quite fifty, but I believe that he was at least ten years less than that. On occasion he could be as boyish as any one, and though there was a suggestion of latent grimness about his expression in repose, his smile was irresistible.

The others, too, soon began to take shape as distinct personalities. First I must name Damar Sing, also older and more sedate than the rest, who

GROUP AT TIMORSHIM.

came as a surveyor and plane-tabler, and gave Longstaff invaluable assistance in that capacity. He was a man of high skill and intelligence, and his map of the mountains surrounding the Rishi and Bagini valleys was a beautiful piece of draughtsmanship. I was advised to choose him as the best subject on whom to practise myself in conversational Hindustani, but, unfortunately, he was a taciturn person, and not very responsive. This was certainly in part due to ill-health; he was very unwell when we first met him at Almora, and though he picked up later, and worked as hard and as willingly as any one, the disease to which he succumbed must have had hold of him throughout the journey, and it was with sincere regret that I heard of his death soon after my return to England.

Then, there was a delightful trio, whom I always mentally bracketed together as the Three Musketeers: Kul Bahadur, tall and slight, with straight well-cut features, that might have belonged to a European, and an interesting rather melancholy face—a youthful Athos; he lacked the sturdy toughness of the other two, but was a neat and nimble rock-climber. An Aramis was lacking, but either Buddhi Chand or Dhan Lal would have made an admirable Porthos. Burly and muscular, great weight-carriers, and good steady goers over any sort of ground, they did yeoman service later in the passage of the Bagini pass.

Buddhi Chand's large impassive countenance always reminded me of a Chinaman; Dhan Lal, heavy jowled, and rather sleepy-looking, one discovered by degrees to be a heaven-born clown. It was first borne in upon me when I saw him dance. They would all, Kharbir and Damar Sing included, take a turn at dancing, of an evening, to some queer melody crooned by the rest in chorus—dancing of the Oriental type, with very little leg movement, and much play with the arms and hands; it was regarded in all cases as more or less of a joke, but Dhan Lal's lumbering motions were subtly instinct with the genius of caricature, and accompanied by grimaces that would have made his fortune on the music-hall stage.

These five, and a bright little person called Ranbir, who took charge of the base camp, when occasion required, were the most prominent during our stay in Garhwal.

The route to Pana on the far side of the valley of the Bireh Ganga, bore a great resemblance to that from Wan to Ramni, but led through more varied and interesting scenery. Working up the valley from Ramni through forests of oak and rhododendron, the latter nearly at their best, and getting occasional glimpses of Trisul, we reached a low pass from which the Kuari ridge, and over it Kamet and its attendant peaks, were visible. Crossing a wooded summit-plateau, the track, still working up-stream towards the point where the two upper branches of the main valley meet, descends steeply through magnificent forests, which extorted a meed of admiration even from Bruce, who had, up till now, been making invidious comparisons with Kashmir. Chesnuts, oaks, and a great variety of other deciduous trees showed an astonishing mixture of hues, the fresh greens of spring mingling with mellow brown and reddish tints which recalled an English autumn: immense paluda pines shot up far above them. As the slope eased off towards the bottom, the forest floor became thickly carpeted with white peonies,

which contrasted strikingly with the rich red of the rhododendrons.

Crossing the two streams which join just below to form the Bireh Ganga, we emerged into the pitiless sun, and toiled for a long hour up the bare northern slope. Our forest spread far up and down the valley, presenting a wonderful surface of soft, harmoniously-blended colours, pierced by whole regiments of dark paluda pines. The hugeness and solidity of the place had a certain impressiveness, but it was too tightly packed to provide a really beautiful valley view. A conspicuous feature in the landscape was a long light-coloured gash in a rock face ahead of us; it was the scar left by a big landslip which took place about ten years ago, and formed a lake of considerable dimensions. The lake still remains, though diminished in size, and we had a partial view of it as we neared Pana.

A little over an hour's walk from Pana the solid contours of the valley are broken by a deep, densely-wooded glen; a cirque of steep rugged cliffs sweeps round it, and at the head of it is the Kuari pass. Turning up this glen we came to a place where, on their return journey two years before, the Brocherels had a fleeting glimpse of what was probably a tiger;[1] and passed a remarkable gorge and waterfall, which have been graphically described by Graham. It was partly choked, and its picturesqueness much impaired by great masses of dirty avalanche snow. The camping-ground of Phul Cheena, at the tree limit, just below the col, is an easy day's march from Pana.

Longstaff, who had started out early with Kul Bahadur to try for a tahr, joined us soon after our arrival, unsuccessful, but very much pleased with his companion. The ice-axes were now unpacked, climbing boots got out, and fervent hopes uttered for fine weather on the morrow.

Nothing could have been more effectively arranged for scenic purposes than this passage of the Kuari pass on May 5. None of us knew what was coming, for Longstaff's previous crossing had been made in mist and torrents of rain. There is a fair zigzag path up

[1] They are not often met with so far up on the mountains, but Mr. Davis had shot one a few years before in very nearly the same spot.

PANORAMA FROM THE KUACI PASS

PANORAMA FROM THE KUARI PASS

the steep little pitch leading to the col, but it was obliterated by hard-frozen snow, and the extemporised route kept one's muscles and mind on the stretch for a good hour. Then a single stride, and I was gazing at a panorama that made one catch one's breath. The day was clear and cloudless, and a brilliant sun illumined every detail of a bewildering multitude of mountains, of every variety of shape and outline, but all alike bold, steep, and formidable, an army of Dents Blanches, Aiguilles Vertes, and Schreckhorns. This was the first overwhelming impression; after trying to absorb the general effect of the scene, one turned to the map for particulars, and made out the stupendous white wall of Kedarnath closing the western extremity of the array, and near it a huge, somewhat isolated pyramid, belonging to the Badrinath group; but then came a confused and confusing crowd of peaks, extending eastward in what seemed to be a solid mass, till they were brought to an end by the great trench of the Dhauli sweeping round to the north. The valley of the Vishnu showed as a mere dark cleft, running up in the direction of Kamet, which stood commanding and dominant far away in the background. Of the rivers themselves nothing at all was visible. On the far side of the Dhauli, in solitary magnificence, rose Dunagiri, the only mountain in sight which had endured a serious attack by mountaineering man.

The coolies were wending their way cautiously over the snow: I hastened on to a projecting knob, where Inderbinen was waiting for me with the camera. He too was intoxicated with the splendour of the scene, which he talked of for days afterwards. He was busily engaged, partly in sizing up the peaks in front of him professionally, and coming to the conclusion that they were, one and all, uncommonly difficult, partly in reconstructing his idea of the Himalaya. I learned that the one which prevailed among the

Zermatt guides, and which he had shared till recently, was that they consisted of a great expanse of hills of moderate size, with three or four very lofty isolated mountains far apart from each other, easy to reach but difficult to ascend, owing to their enormous height. How this notion grew up I do not know; possibly Asia may have got confused with Africa, of which the above is a more or less true description: perhaps the paucity of *names* has had something to do with it.

That there should be hundreds of great mountains unnamed and unknown, extending over 2000 miles or so, is a conception which could not be got into a Swiss guide's head without considerable difficulty. As Inderbinen put it, he had no idea there were so many mountains in the world. I gave him another shock by telling him that the Kuari pass was not a glacier pass—or even a snow-pass; that when Longstaff had crossed it two years ago it was covered with long grass, and we should find it in a similar condition on our return.

Some excellent glissades soon brought us to the edge of the woods, where we sat down to enjoy a picturesque prospect of the more southerly summits of the Kamet range, charmingly framed by the trees. Here, too, I first made acquaintance with "curry pups," a delectable species of mutton pie, one of Dina's masterpieces. Dina is Bruce's cook; he performed his important duties with distinguished success, often under conditions of extreme difficulty and discomfort. After tiffin came a drop of two hours to Tapoban, so steep that we did not get a sight of the village till we were within a mile of it, and almost at the level of the bottom of the valley.

There is a fine view from Tapoban of the pyramidal Badrinath peak, but its immediate surroundings are not attractive; like most places in the Dhauli valley, it is windy and dusty, and there is no shade. Nevertheless the off-day, which we were at last allowed, was welcomed by every one. The arrival in the Dhauli valley marked the end of a stage which, though quite uneventful, had been very enjoyable; in fact, so far as simple enjoyment went, these ten days were probably the most unmitigatedly pleasant that I spent in

Garhwal. Everything was still before us. We had not yet reached altitudes which affect one adversely; the life was extraordinarily stimulating, and the novelty and interest of each day's march provided an excitement little inferior to that of actual mountaineering.

I felt stronger and healthier every day, and indeed believed, innocently but sincerely, that I was in perfect training. In such conditions one recaptures much of the charm which pervades the subalpine literature of fifty or sixty years ago, and which has vanished from the Alps for ever.

We were now within a short walk of the Rishi valley, and at length local knowledge of a more or less definite character became available with regard to the "back-door" by which the difficulty or impossibility of effecting a direct entrance into it can be circumvented. There was, it appeared, a place called Darashi, high up on the northern side, to which sheep were regularly taken during the summer months by a track which crossed the northern boundary ridge near the mouth of the river. The reports which we had previously heard with regard to this back-door entrance were vague and conflicting, but the information now obtained sounded promising, and we looked forward hopefully to being inside the mysterious valley in the course of a few days.

## CHAPTER V

### LATA KHARAK

WE resumed our way on May 7, passing a hot spring in which Graham bathed in 1883; but I found the water so hot that I could not keep my fingers in it for more than two or three seconds. The scenery was very Swiss in character, save for the great size of the paluda pines on the hillside that we had just descended. I mentally compared it at the time to a dull stretch in the Rhone valley, but when I went down the Rhone valley in the following November, I withdrew the comparison; I found that it struck me as much more open and rounded than it used to look. The sense of the greater steepness and narrowness of the Himalayan valleys was already losing the sharpness of a first impression. Above Tapoban the valley gradually closes in and, where the Rishi river debouches, narrows into a regular gorge, spanned by a picturesque bridge. Just beyond the bridge there is a waterfall; I found mention of it by Graham, and discovered it in one of my own photographs, but I had entirely forgotten it. Waterfalls are not a feature of Himalayan, as they are of Swiss, landscape; there are surprisingly few of them, and when they do occur, their effect is almost always utterly insignificant.

One could see a considerable distance up the Rishi valley, but no signs were visible of the difficulties which bar all progress a little farther on. Longstaff hankered

after an attempt to force the passage; but I doubt if the game would be worth the candle.

Above the gorge the valley opens out again, into the camping-place of Towa (two and a half easy hours from Tapoban), a bare dreary spot, from which we proposed to start for the "back-door" into the Rishi valley. The rest of the day was fully occupied with the redistribution of stores, etc.

In the afternoon a shikari called Bhop Chand presented himself, who had been recommended to us by Mr. Davis at Almora; he said he was also the man who had accompanied Graham and Emil Boss into the Rishi valley, and produced a chit, signed by them, speaking in the warmest terms of his pluck and fidelity. We engaged him at once, and Longstaff and I started with him next morning at 7.15, on the ascent to Lata Kharak, the first stage on the way to Darashi, the coolies having got under weigh some time earlier. Bruce remained behind to look after some thirty more who ought to have come on the day before from Tapoban, but had not appeared. We passed above the cultivated terraces of Lata village, and, in a couple of hours, overtook the main body; the track turned straight up through a forest of pines, and then began a dreary time. The going was very bad; steep and slippery, altogether a harder piece of work than any one had anticipated. Longstaff delivered a harangue, and promised bakshish, but the men had to be coaxed and hustled to their feet after their frequent rests, one by one, and by the time the last stragglers had been set going, the leaders, perhaps three hundred yards farther on, would be settling down again, and forming the nucleus of a fresh halt. When this stage is reached a Job-like patience is required; but I could not help feeling considerable sympathy for the men, of whom many were, obviously, very tired indeed; considering their physique, and the indifferent nourishment on which they habitually subsist, I think the Garhwali porters, as a rule, went surprisingly well. This was quite the most trying experience of the kind that we had; none of our other marches involved such a severe and unrelieved ascent.

COOLIES AT MALARI.

Towards mid-day I began to feel weak with hunger myself, and was very glad to munch a big hunk of ghur supplied me by Buddhi Chand. At last, a little before two o'clock, the whole caravan was assembled at Lata Kharak, on the top of a ridge dividing the Rishi and Dhauli valleys, and separated from the main mass of the northern wall of the Rishi gorge by a narrow cleft of extreme steepness, at the head of which was the pass by which we proposed to make our entrance.

The ridge grew rapidly narrower, and terminated about a mile away in Lata peak (12,624 feet), just in the angle made by the junction of the two rivers. The camping-ground was a trifle higher, a little above the tree-level, and snow lay everywhere several inches deep.

In a very few minutes tents were pitched; loads stacked and covered up; the coolies had disappeared downhill amongst the trees; and, tiffin disposed of, everybody set to work on building a big shelter for Dina's cooking operations. A cold wind was blowing up from the south-west, and a battle royal between sun and clouds raged the whole afternoon. The clouds had rather the best of it, and occasional storms of sleet swept by, but the fine intervals were filled with a succession of superb pictures, in the manner of Elijah Walton at his wildest.

Dunagiri was now close at hand, and the southern ridges of the Kamet range, seen from a slightly different angle, looked even sharper and more jagged than from the Kuari pass; the crests too of the great northern buttresses of Trisul, which shut in the Rishi, were visible from the camp, and—a spectacle at least equally impressive—the gloomy depths of the Dhauli valley.

Suddenly, to our surprise, Bruce appeared, having raced up in the amazingly short time of three and a quarter hours. The missing thirty had stayed at Tapoban because *one* of them was ill! However, the remaining twenty-nine came on to Towa early in the morning, and were now following on. They duly arrived in the course of the afternoon, and we were now within reach of the "back-door" of the Rishi, with ample supplies for some weeks.

At this point there occurs in my diary the brief entry, "*Horrible* night." There are only meagre details, but my recollection of it is still extraordinarily vivid. In the first place, I was reminded painfully and repeatedly of a passage which I had recently read in a paper on Himalayan travel by Colonel Michell: "On one occasion I camped out for a week at an elevation of 18,200 feet; the only inconvenience I felt was oppressiveness in breathing when sleeping at night. This I found was owing to the recumbent position of the body, which seemed to choke the lungs; I awoke every twenty minutes, and had to stand up and get them into working order again. After a time I learnt to sleep with my back propped up almost upright. This was a great relief, and I slept much easier afterwards."[1]

Though we were much lower, my experience on this occasion was almost precisely similar, except that I stopped short at sitting up in order to recover my breath. The actual physical discomfort, however,

[1] *Alpine Journal*, vol. xi. p. 207.

was not very great; the feature of the case that I wish specially to emphasise was the overwhelming and unendurable feeling of mental depression that accompanied it. I was utterly cowed and miserable, and spent my recurring periods of wakefulness in abjectly regretting my folly in ever having come out. I believe also that one of my eyes worried me a good deal, but my recollection of that has entirely faded. I was sharing a tent with Longstaff; when I poured out my woes to him next morning, he was very cheering and consolatory, gave me some eye-wash, which was speedily effectual, and told me that no one ever went for a prolonged expedition without having, at some time or other, an attack of depression, during which he wished he had never started; only no one ever owns up to it afterwards. Of course it is easy to say that low spirits are a natural accompaniment of a wakeful and uncomfortable night, and therefore not worth dwelling upon: and if this experience had stood entirely by itself, I should probably have acted on that view. Two or three things, however, have combined to induce me to go deliberately to the opposite extreme. I had only once before spent a night at anything like the same elevation, at the highest camp reached during my visit to Ruwenzori with Mr. Freshfield in 1905. The height of this camp was very nearly the same as that of Lata Kharak. On that occasion too I had suffered in exactly the same way, though much less acutely, from difficulty in breathing; and also, though with less violence, was gripped by the same senseless unaccountable feeling of utter discouragement, the memory of which remained with me as of something novel and uncanny. So I was a good deal impressed when next day at Lata Kharak I found that Inderbinen too had had a bad night, accompanied by a degree of depression, which struck him as unusual and odd; "I felt afraid," he said. Most of the recorded statements of others on this subject refer only to purely bodily symptoms, or to depression of spirits in general terms; but I have recently come across one or two that are worth citing: De Saussure, quoted by Longstaff in his monograph on *Mountain Sickness*, uses the emphatic phrase "indescribable uneasiness"; and Mr. J. F. Cheetham gives the following account of his "first experience of the unpleasant effects which highly rarefied atmosphere, inclement weather, and severe exertion combine to produce at great elevations. Giddiness, acute headache, nausea, were the more specific sensations, agreeably superadded to *a general feeling of intense misery*, and profound mental and physical depression."[1]

Fortunately, in this particular respect, the first experience is apt to be the last. Perhaps I have made too much of it; but, after all, such descriptions, however vague and unscientific they may be, are the raw material of the knowledge that there is such a thing as mountain sickness at all; possibly too some future victim, having read this one, may be aided to grin and bear it in a more philosophical spirit than I did.

The Brocherels, Bhop Chand, and a couple of

[1] *Alpine Journal*, vol. iii. p. 137. Cp. Younghusband, *The Heart of a Continent*, p. 224.

PANORAMA FROM THE PEAK NEAR LATA KHARAK

PANORAMA FROM THE PEAK NEAR LATA KHARAK

Gurkhas started out to have a look at the pass to Darashi, while Longstaff and Damar Sing went down to Lata peak and did some surveying. Neither Bruce nor I felt disposed to go anywhere, and my principal exercise during the day consisted in changing into and out of a Shetland waistcoat as intervals of scorching sun alternated with spells of driving cloud and mist and bitterly cold wind. Bhop Chand returned in a very short time and informed Bruce that there was far too much snow on the pass for loaded coolies, and that the way in would not be open for a month. This estimate was startling, but it was fully borne out by the event. We did, in fact, not get in till three weeks later, and then the way was far from being passable, according to the coolies' standard, as will be seen.

Not only was there a great deal of snow, but it did not at present show any signs of going. Bruce could find nothing to say for the weather except that it was all wrong. It was very hard on him that his excellent arrangements should be thwarted like this. I turned to the map for inspiration, and suggested going on to the big valley on the other side of Dunagiri and the Bagini glacier, which looked quite capable of giving us occupation for weeks. Meanwhile the others came in; we were surprised at an absurdly early hour by the announcement of dinner, and dined at about 3.45, in a snowstorm; then a council of war was held. To have marched all the stores and tents up such a hill merely to march them down again was a lame and impotent conclusion from which the more strenuous spirits shrank. Was it practicable for us and the five Gurkhas to go in carrying as much as possible, and then return for more loads of provisions? No one could say how many days this course would require: it might be ten, it might be even more, and we should be consuming the said provisions during most of the time. Clearly this would not do. Finally, the fact was swallowed that we had made a false start; the move to Lata Kharak should have been preceded by a reconnaissance from below; and, in fine, we must retrace our steps. The Bagini glacier was so obviously the next best place to go that it was decided upon at once: I don't think any alternative was suggested: Dunagiri was hard by, but there was too much recent snow for an attempt on so lofty a mountain.

In order that the grind up should not be wholly wasted, we went next morning up a little peak between the camp and the pass, overlooking the cleft already mentioned and the bad bit on the way from the pass to Darashi, and spent a long hour on the top, which I should be very sorry to have missed. This was one of our great views, scarcely if at all inferior to that from the Kuari pass. With Dunagiri and the range on the other side of the Dhauli we were already on familiar terms, but the magnificence of the prospect on the side of the Rishi valley surpassed all expectation. Nanda Devi, now seen for the first time, was in full view, standing quite alone, and looking every inch of its immense height. Though Trisul itself was scarcely visible, the graceful summit of its northern buttress, point 20,842, crowned most effectively the savage mountain mass which overhangs the Rishi, now glittering with freshly-fallen snow. I was lucky enough to secure a series of photographs embracing the whole panorama. They show what we saw, but give only a faint idea of the effect of those miles of blinding white splendour. The descent was one long and excellent

glissade; and it was refreshing to watch the enjoyment of the Gurkhas, to all of whom, except Kharbir, glissading was a novelty.

The following day we descended direct to Surai Thota, three miles above Towa; the main camp had been already moved up there, and there it remained till June 19. Surai Thota lies at the entrance to the Tolma glen, at the head of which the icy slopes of Dunagiri are visible. It was by way of the Tolma glen that Graham made his attempt on Dunagiri. The camping-ground is a dusty windy disagreeable place, but decidedly preferable to Towa, besides being a much better starting-point for the pass into the Rishi valley.

The limits of the forest region were near. As one proceeds up the Niti road the Dhauli valley opens out gaunt and bare, with a broad stony floor, but the scenery is very striking in a wild grim style; only up some of the narrow lateral glens running up towards the spurs of Dunagiri one got occasional glimpses of dark densely-wooded slopes. It is a great misfortune in such a region as this not to be something of a geologist: one misses as much as one does in a strange city through not knowing the language; but it was apparent to the most ignorant eye that these glens were in the backward condition belonging to mountains geologically "new," and that the processes which have carved out and rounded off the valleys of the Alps were here very incomplete. Their mouths are mere slits in the vast faces of naked cliff that tower above the Dhauli.

The road was full of life and movement, for somewhere about here—I do not know where the exact line should be drawn—is the limit of continuous occupation. Joshimath, fourteen or fifteen miles below Surai Thota, is certainly inhabited all the year round, but most if not all the villages higher up than Joshimath are abandoned every year about the end of October, and

The DHAULI VALLEY.

remain empty till the following May. The tide of annual migration was now at the flood, and we were repeatedly engulfed by caravans of men, women, children, oxen, yaks, ponies, sheep, and goats, all carrying burdens of some kind, except "babies in arms," who reposed in baskets on their mothers' backs. Civilisation in Garhwal has not yet arrived at jewel cases, and the women carried all their ornaments on their persons, principally necklaces, strings of coins, and, in some instances, large nose-rings, with stones and coloured glass in them; they appeared to be wearing their smartest clothes as well, and some of them attained a considerable degree of rude picturesqueness. As a rule they left the path and turned their backs while we were passing; but the amount of conscientiousness displayed in this matter varied a good deal. The costume of the men was severely plain and practical; the only note of colour was the head-dress, a red fez, or a dark green skull-cap with a red border being the commonest varieties. One met some pathetic little parties, in which there were very few sheep or other animals, and the women displayed no ornaments, and the men were in rags; but the greater number seemed to belong to the ranks of the well-to-do.

These sheep, of which we consumed a considerable number, were wiry little creatures, and there was not much to be said for them considered as mutton. But in this country they are scarcely looked upon in that light at all. First and foremost they are esteemed as producers of an annual crop of wool; their second important function is that of beasts of burden, and they were rarely to be seen on the road without their two compact little bags of salt or borax slung across their backs, each bag containing five pounds' weight at least.

Scenically, this portion of the Niti road ends and culminates in an imposing fashion at the camping-ground of Juma Gwar. The great rock walls close in upon the stream on both sides; passing through the narrow portal one is at once hemmed in by an oval of tall pine-clad cliffs opening out at the upper end, and cut through on the right bank of the river by the torrent descending from the Juma glacier. The camping-place is on a little tongue of elevated ground between the two streams. It was more like a bit of the gorge of the Sutjeska in Bosnia than anything else I have seen; to Bruce it recalled the Astor country, and he then and there developed a scheme for finishing up by a high-level journey to Astor, and on to Abbottabad, *via* Chilas and Khagan.

On emerging from the gorge of Juma Gwar we crossed to the left bank of the Dhauli and entered the Dunagiri valley through the village of Ruing, an amazingly picturesque little place nestling under some fine deodars. Here we separated for a time; Bruce, with his usual good nature, proceeded up the Dunagiri valley in charge of the main caravan, while Longstaff and I went off with Kharbir, Bhop Chand, and Kul Bahadur for some tahr and barhal shooting up a little glen which joins the main valley just above the village. Our march was a very short one, but I could scarcely crawl to the

JUMA GWAR.

end of it, and collapsed completely for forty-eight hours: there was nothing wrong; it was like convalescence after a long illness, when one feels well but hopelessly weak; and, except that such a state of things opened up rather dismal possibilities for the future, I was perfectly comfortable and happy. Was this the remains of

mountain sickness? I cannot account for it in any other way, and the most violent effects do often seem to proceed from the first attack. I shall never forget the untiring devotion with which Kul Bahadur looked to my comfort during these two days.

There was a tiny little hamlet called Garpag perched on a crag opposite the camp, of which the whole population save two households had been destroyed by an epidemic a few years earlier. The survivors lived on, surrounded by the desolate habitations of their former neighbours, now rapidly falling into ruin.

Both tahr (a species of wild goat) and barhal (wild sheep) are mountaineers, but their tastes, like those of other mountaineers, differ: the barhal likes fairly easy going, and has no objection to snowfields, whereas the tahr is passionately devoted to difficult rock climbs, and cares very little for anything else, insomuch that it is possible to predict pretty confidently by mere inspection of a mountain-side whether tahr or barhal will be found on it. They are rarely or never met with on the same ground. There are members of the climbing world at home who would like to see a similar separation of the sheep from the goats established in the Alps.

Natural affinity led Longstaff in pursuit of the tahr, and, after two days' hard work he secured a couple of pretty good heads, though in truth a tahr's head does not make much of a show as a trophy, unless the mask and beard can be preserved along with it, and they are principally valued because of the well-known difficulty of getting near them. I was sufficiently revived by that time to go out with Kharbir and Bhop Chand and try for a barhal, but my efforts did not meet with success. It was not the fault of Kharbir or Bhop Chand. Neither was it the fault of the barhal.

This was the only occasion on which the claims of the mountains were postponed to sport; such shooting

LATA KHARAK

as was done or attempted later was all for the sake of the meat-supply. On the fourth day (May 17) we crossed into the Dunagiri valley, descending just above Dunagiri village, and rejoined the main body on a pleasant boulder-strewn meadow, about half a mile from the snout of the great Bagini glacier.

# CHAPTER VI

## THE BAGINI GLACIER

We were now all assembled within easy reach of the ice-world; during two days of indifferent weather little was done except some plane-tabling, and much time was spent in debating the question, What to do next? If we had arrived in the Bagini valley without any preoccupations, we might well have stayed there for weeks, and in that case our list of peaks actually climbed would probably have been lengthened. The Brocherels were eager to attempt at least one of the many lofty summits surrounding the valley before leaving it. Here were the peaks, they were big, they were difficult, no one had been up them; what more could anybody want? Such was their attitude, and, speaking generally, I am now more and more inclined to think that it is the one most likely to produce actual results in a strange country, but the turn which the deliberations actually took led to so brilliant a success that it was more than justified.

Bruce and the guides had already been on the glacier with some of the Gurkhas, with some idea of giving the latter a lesson in ice-work. No place was found at all suited for this purpose, but they had been far enough up the glacier to see round the corner to the south, and had observed an apparently practicable col; the glacier provided an easy highway to the foot of it, along which loaded coolies could be taken.

The Bagini glacier is an ice-stream of great size; starting in an easterly direction, then turning nearly due north, and again turning back sharply W.N.W., it encloses on three sides a great spur which stretches northward from Dunagiri. Its course is well and correctly shown on the G.T.S. map, except in one particular. The map represents it as extending well beyond this northern spur, and joining a smaller glacier which descends to the west of the spur. The accuracy of this representation at the time is confirmed by General Macintyre, who some forty years ago camped at Dunagiri village in the course of a shooting trip, reached the foot of the glacier in an hour's sharp walking, and then went "up one of Doonagiri glaciers—for there are two which unite."[1] But long before 1907 both glaciers had receded a very considerable distance, and our camp was well above the place where the former junction must have taken place.

Clearly the col which had been noted on the southern boundary ridge ought—supposing it would "go" on the other side—to lead into the Rishi valley; and the Rishi valley still absorbed most of our thoughts. Could we not best turn the situation to account by attempting a reconnaissance of the upper part of it from this side? This was the question upon which the dis-

[1] *Hindu Koh: Wanderings and Wild Sport on and beyond the Himalayas*, p. 409.

cussion finally centred. It was brought to an end by an announcement from Bruce that he had a plan—a plan which would provide a very sporting and interesting expedition and solve other difficulties as well; "and," he concluded, pointing a menacing forefinger in my direction, "I 'm going to sacrifice—you!"

I professed myself ready, and he proceeded to unfold his scheme: he, Longstaff, the Brocherels, and four Gurkhas (Kharbir and the Three Musketeers) would start with provisions for seven or eight days, and the lightest possible kit in the way of tents and bedding, and thus equipped try the col. If the map could be relied upon, it was clear that the descent must end in the great glacier basin already described which surrounds the base of Nanda Devi, and that the way into the Rishi valley would lie through the narrow chasm by which the Rishi river makes its exit. This might turn out to be impassable, but, at the worst, they could always return on their tracks, and a visit to the Nanda Devi basin would be well worth making.[1]

On the other hand, once in the main Rishi valley they would be on ground previously reached by Graham and Davis, and would be able somehow to find a way out.

To Longstaff, the prospect of going for several days with an unusually heavy load, scanty fare, and limited tent accommodation, was irresistibly attractive, and success, if achieved, would in Bruce's opinion be further

[1] It is interesting to speculate on what would have been the result of the expedition if the map had been correct in this respect. In the light of subsequently acquired knowledge, it seems not improbable that retreat would have been necessary; as, if they had been unable to get through the chasm, their provisions would have hardly been sufficient for a search for another way over.

The Bagini Glacier

valuable on account of the moral effect of it on the native mind. Not only shikaris, he said, but ordinary coolies too, believed in the bottom of their hearts that they were better men on a hillside than sahibs, and if the party got through it would make a powerful impression, and render much easier the task of persuading a sufficient number of men to face the passage into the Rishi valley. Such a party could not afford to take any one who was not able to take his full share of the loads. I have had little training as a weight-carrier, and should probably have felt obliged to stand out, even if I had been at my best; but I was not really fit, and rather welcomed the prospect of taking things easily for a time.

The weather mended somewhat during the morning of May 19, and preparations were made for a start on the morrow. It snowed and hailed again towards evening, but on the 20th, having decided not to go far and to camp comfortably on the right-hand moraine, we started in leisurely fashion at 9.30, with four Mummery tents. After three hours' easy going, principally along beds of snow lying between the hillside and the moraine, a very fair camping-place was found on the latter, nearly opposite the angle where the glacier makes its second turn. The Dunagiri spur terminated in a horse-shoe of dark precipices, embracing a small glacier whose broken surface was robbed of its pictorial effect through being deeply covered with snow. But the day was dull and cloudy, and dry pellets of snow, like a fine hail, began to fall as the afternoon wore on. It was not till the next day that the great glory of the

Bagini glacier was revealed to us—its majestic eastern wall. This is a truly noble piece of natural architecture, uniform in design but never monotonous, as the boundaries of so many of these great ice-streams are apt to be, a row of peaks massive in structure but

soaring in outline, connected by curtains of extreme steepness, the whole being veiled and draped with a dazzling garment of snow and hanging glacier.

One of the matters of high policy which had been much debated when we were all together in England was the question of early starts. Bruce argued that they were a mistake; not only was there the risk of frost-bite to be taken into account, but long exposure to the intense cold of the small hours, when one's vitality was at its lowest, reduced one's energy so much as fully to counterbalance the gain in point of time. Longstaff concurred in this doctrine, and I welcomed it with unabashed satisfaction. But on this—the first occasion which arose for putting it into practice—instructions were given in an entirely opposite sense, and after a breakfast consisting of two or three cups of hot chocolate, we got under weigh a little before five o'clock. Those who were bound for the pass were carrying tremendous loads—primus stoves, petroleum, cooking-pots, tents, sleeping-bags, instruments, rifles and ammunition, a large supply of ropes, and provisions for ten days.

Crossing the glacier in forty-five minutes, we were round the corner in an hour, and Henri Brocherel pointed out the col to me, just to the right of an immense pale brown mountain powdered with snow, and with the most incredible hanging glaciers on it. This was Changabang, the A 21 of the G.T.S. map (22,516 feet); with its splendid precipices rising above the col, the great eastern wall comes to an abrupt and imposing end. The foregoing description of it was scribbled at the time; Longstaff wrote of it later, "Changabang is the most superbly beautiful mountain I have ever seen; its north-west face, a sheer precipice of over 5000 feet, being composed of such pale granite that it is at first taken for snow lying on the cliffs at an impossibly steep angle."

It was chilly, and I thought we should never get clear of the shadow cast by the great eastern peaks, but about 7.45 Inderbinen and I reached the sunshine not far from the foot of the steep snow-slope leading to the col, and waited there for the heavily-laden main body. I spent most of the time in pounding my numbed feet with my ice-axe to restore circulation,

hammering extra savagely at the left one, which remained impervious to all my efforts.

Here we could see right up the whole of the remaining stretch of the glacier; a small but well-defined snow-peak rose immediately above the col on the west; beyond it the snow-covered névé, sloping gently upwards to the western extremity of the glacier basin, approached gradually nearer to the level of the southern boundary ridge, and it was evident that farther on in that direction there was a way up to the ridge much easier than the ascent to the col just in front of us. So an hour later I moved on with Inderbinen, who soon afterwards deposited his rucksack and our eatables under a stone. We had no doubt that we should reach the ridge, and speed the others on their way down into the Rishi valley. It looked like an

easy and not very prolonged stroll. Everybody knows the deceptiveness of these undulating stretches of unbroken whiteness, but never have I been so completely taken in as on this occasion. We seemed to make no headway, and the slopes always looked as if they were going to subside into a level plateau, but never did.

Looking back at the others toiling along far behind under their heavy loads, Inderbinen prophesied that they would not cross the pass to-day. Presently he began stopping for two or three minutes, at very short intervals, to get his breath, and progress soon became so slow that I decided to abandon the attempt to reach the ridge. I was not at all affected by difficulty in breathing, but rather leg weary, extremely hungry, and quite willing to turn back.

The others had already fulfilled Inderbinen's prediction, and selected a camping-ground by some big blocks of stone at a height of 18,300 feet. We walked clean past them almost beyond shouting distance before we realised where they were. Longstaff hallooed an invitation to stay and spend the night with them; it was a seductive one, and made in a most generous spirit, but to take advantage of it meant encroaching on their meagre sleeping accommodation and making an inroad on their slender stock of provisions; this was not to be thought of, so we pursued our way back to the rucksack, and had our first square meal. The heat and glare of the sun were terrific. I have never experienced anything like it, before or since. Inderbinen, for the first time in his life, spent the night smarting with the sting of it, and next day his skin was burnt nearly black, and coming off rapidly. I fared much better, being, by this time, thickly protected by whiskers and beard. The snow grew soft lower down, and it was a laborious walk back to the moraine camp, where the coolies were waiting for us (3.20). We had a big drink, the first liquid since breakfast; the tents were taken down and packed, and we went on. The sun had wrought an extraordinary transformation in the route by which we had come; the snow was giving way everywhere, and in the middle of the beds along

THE BAGINI GLACIER

which we had marched up a turbid yellow torrent was now streaming.

We reached the main camp at about six o'clock, and it was only after our arrival that I discovered that my left foot was frost-bitten. Whether the pounding I had given it in the morning contributed to the result, I cannot say ; but I was hopelessly crippled

for two days. This was more than a temporary misfortune, as it compelled me to forego a photographing expedition on the ridge above the camp, and Bruce, who had visited it when barhal hunting, pronounced the view of Dunagiri equal to anything we had seen. I hobbled painfully down to Juma Gwar on the 24th, discharging some of my pent-up photographic energy on the village of Ruing and its inhabitants, and regained the main camp at Surai Thota the next day. On the 27th I went up the Tolma valley to try for a tahr. Soon after two o'clock I heard some of the men shouting, and was summoned to come with the glasses and inspect something moving up the valley. Some animal? No—human beings; and for a moment the idea crossed my mind that some sportsman had taken possession of the valley, and wanted to know what I was doing on his ground; but they followed the road to Tolma village, and as they tramped wearily by, far below, deaf and impervious to my shouts and signals, I recognised, with a throb of gladness, of which the intensity startled me, that it was the Bagini party.

CHANGABANG.

# CHAPTER VII

## THE BAGINI PASS

To the Bagini party it is now time to return. Again all previous good resolutions were thrown to the winds; they started on May 22 at 4.30 A.M., but soon had to stop on account of cold feet, and it was probably at this time that Kharbir was frost-bitten. The ridge was reached very near the western extremity of the glacier basin, and the ascent to it turned out to be a good deal steeper and more troublesome than it had looked from below; the final slopes were frozen hard, the rope had to be used, and a good deal of step-cutting was necessary. It was ten o'clock when they stood on the crest of the pass, at a height of 20,100 feet. It must have been hard to forego a leisurely study of the surroundings, but the descent to a vast *firn*, shut in by snow-clad peaks, looked so formidable that they did not venture to linger. Longstaff, however, had time to secure excellent photographs of what must have been by far the most striking objects in the panorama: Dunagiri on the west towering 3000 feet above them, and on the east Changabang, the peak which had so strongly excited our admiration on the previous day. Seen from this standpoint the latter mountain shows a south-eastern arête, which certainly looks as if it might be climbed, and I think it was the appearance of this arête which led Longstaff to the belief that Graham was right in

identifying with Changabang the mountain which he ascended and called Mount Monal.

Though I could not get Alexis to admit it, the passage down the snow-draped cliffs was very difficult, by far the most formidable piece of mountaineering accomplished during the whole of our stay in Garhwal. Iron *pitons* were used freely, and by means of fixing these into cracks in the rocks and doubling ropes round them, they succeeded in effecting the descent, but each man and each load had to be let down separately. At one time as much as two hundred feet of doubled rope was out at once. Alexis occupied the responsible post of last man, and successfully accomplished the difficult task of bringing all the ropes along with him. The fact that they took more than five hours in descending about 1000 feet speaks for itself, though, of course, if they had only been carrying ordinary Alpine loads they would have moved faster. They got no farther than the foot of the pass that day, and camped on the névé at 4 P.M., at a height of 18,800 feet. There they spent a cold and uncomfortable night, Bruce in particular suffering from an attack of mountain sickness.

Next morning (May 28) they proceeded down a large snow-covered glacier in a south-easterly direction, with the twin peaks of Nanda Devi showing over the ridge straight ahead of them.

They had already discovered that they were not in the great Nanda Devi basin, and it was now apparent that they were a long distance to the west of it, and that the map here was quite unreliable. The glacier which they were now descending had not only never been visited, but its very existence was unknown. It flowed at right angles into a second glacier, for which the name Rhamani or Arhamani was afterwards given us by the shikari. They turned sharply down it, their direction being now south-west. The rest of their route was in full view of the heights on the south side of the Rishi valley, and the whole of the Arhamani glacier can be seen from the same standpoint, descending from the foot of the more easterly of the two Bagini cols.

This other col, therefore, if practicable, offers a much shorter and more direct route from the Bagini glacier to the Rishi valley than the one actually followed. The descent on the south side is quite short, though steep, and would probably prove easier than that which our party had just effected; but the ascent on the Bagini side is undoubtedly the more difficult of the two.

The end of the Arhamani glacier, "a steep tongue covered with a horribly unstable litter of moraine stuff," was reached at mid-day. "We next came" (Longstaff continues in the *Alpine Journal*) "to an extraordinary gorge cut out by the glacier stream, which was often quite invisible, though very audible, under thick beds of hard snow. In one place we had to lower our loads on the rope, and follow ourselves in a similar manner. After food and a short rest, we broke out of the gorge on the right, climbed up the steep slopes on the west, and down again to the first patch of birch trees, where we camped at 6 P.M. (13,100 feet) amongst enormous boulders, which still held some snowdrifts, from which we could get water.

"To the east towered the cliffs of Nanda Devi, too steep to hold snow. South was the entrance to the Trisuli nala, though the peak itself was invisible. Directly at our feet, more than 1000 feet below, lay the junction of the Arhamani and Rishi torrents, at an altitude of only 11,790 feet, as I determined three weeks later."

The Rishi Valley.
As shown on G.T.S. Map.

The Rishi Valley.
The part enclosed in black lines altered in accordance with Dr. Longstaff's Map.

From this camp they started to traverse the slopes that fall from the peak marked "Niti No. 8, 17,056 feet" on the G.T.S. map, but after only two hours' walking, having shot a couple of barhal, they decided to halt. Longstaff's contemporary note of the next day's march is "a really terrific day coasting along the slopes of Niti peak at about 18,000 feet." From 7.30 A.M. the strata being the wrong way, they were constantly toiling up steep slopes to avoid difficulties, only to find cut-off cliffs on the other side. At length they were gladdened by the sight, far below them, of the grassy alp of Dibrugheta. The true topography of the northern side of the Rishi valley was now apparent, and can be summed up in very few words. Above the hollow where Dibrugheta lies, the slopes of Niti peak descend without any break or interruption to the river: beyond them comes the valley of the Arhamani glacier, lying at the foot of the northern portion of the great transverse block which shuts off the upper Rishi valley from the Nanda Devi basin, and is cut in two by the cleft through which the Rishi makes its way out. The Arhamani torrent meets the Rishi just below the mouth of the cleft. The G.T.S. map shows quite correctly Dibrugheta, the slopes of Niti peak, and the *mouth* of the Arhamani valley, but, quite wrongly, it represents the latter as running up to the southern foot of Dunagiri, and this half of the transverse block as a spur of Dunagiri descending from its highest point; a purely imaginary branch of the Nanda Devi basin appears on its other side enclosed between it and the southern boundary of the Bagini glacier.

One other matter of some interest ought to be mentioned here: the real transverse block, rising steeply above the lower Arhamani valley, reaches its highest point in a snowy peak with a long level top, and then, sinking considerably, comes to an end at the foot of Changabang, close to what I have called the second col and at the same level with it. It is here not much elevated above the upper levels of the Arhamani glacier, and there should be a way over it into the Nanda Devi basin. Longstaff, who has been much nearer to this point than I have, thought the ascent would be difficult, but I am convinced that it offers a likelier way in than the only apparent alternative, the Rishi cleft.

Dibrugheta, and the next camp, Darashi, were two of the stages of our return journey up the valley a few days later, but, owing to a mist, they failed to find the regular track which leads over from Darashi into the Tolma valley, and ended by making a traverse right over the top of a small peak (15,700 feet) to the east of the usual col. This, the highest point on the ridge between the Rishi and Tolma valleys, they christened Tolma peak. It gave some good climbing, and the descent, in snow and a gale of wind, of the snow gullies on the far side at first presented considerable difficulties. Finally, a glissade down old avalanche snow took them into the forest at the head of the Tolma glen.

Not long afterwards, as I have already mentioned, I saw them from the other side of the valley, and early on May 29 I was back at Surai Thota, listening eagerly to the story of their adventures. They were flushed with success, and made light of their hardships, but it was easy to read between the lines that they had had a very rough time. For five days the only water available was melted snow, and on three nights they had no fuel at all. One of Kharbir's feet had been frost-bitten, and it was decidedly fortunate that the early part of the expedition coincided with an unusually unbroken spell of fine weather. As it was, the whole party, with one most regrettable exception, were aboundingly fit and well and eager for more work. The expedition was a magnificent *tour de force* of a kind which is not likely to be often repeated. Indeed, for many years, perhaps one might safely say for generations to come, the difficulty or impossibility of traversing high and difficult passes is likely to remain an outstanding feature of difference between Himalayan exploration and the early exploration of the Alps. For the pioneers of the 'sixties the discovery of a new pass, with a descent over untrodden ground, and amid unforeseeable difficulties, held an attraction little, if at all, inferior to that of the conquest of a new peak. It might be necessary to provide for the chance of a night out, but that once over, a long tramp would suffice to bring the travellers to shelter and food of a more or less civilised kind. It is a different affair altogether when tents and bedding, however scanty, have to be taken along, and provisions for several days certain, with a margin for contingencies. True, there are barhal and other game, but they are an uncertain resource, while rifles, guns, and ammunition form a solid addition to the amount that has to be carried.

I think the Bagini party on this occasion reached about the limit of what is possible, in the way of cutting loose from one's base. It is true that Longstaff has thrown out the idea that some future party might get into the Nanda Devi basin and cross from there into the Milam valley, rejoining their base higher up the Niti road by way of the Girthi valley. But I do not expect to hear of this suggestion being taken up, except perhaps by himself. Practically the crossing from one side to the other of one of the main ranges by a mountaineers' pass is not a workable affair, under present conditions, unless there happens to be an easier pass, which coolies could go over, close by, and such a combination can only occur rarely. An attempt on those lines was made by the Nanga Parbat party, but it did not work out according to expectation.

The ideal method in suitable country would be to have two parties, one on each side of the range, working in combination with each other. It could be quite well carried out by a party of the size of ours, and would not be beyond the resources of the *bandobast* of such a leader as Bruce. The range between the routes to the Mana and Niti passes would be admirably adapted for this kind of treatment.

To return for one moment to the Bagini pass: it ought certainly to be turned to account by any future visitors to the Rishi valley, in order to avoid the irksome necessity of going in and out by the same route. Our recent experiences show that it would be quite feasible, if the track to Darashi were free from snow, to make arrangements for coolies to meet a party coming over from the Bagini glacier, either at Dibrugheta or higher up the valley. It would be an even better plan, and more easily manageable, to utilise the Bagini pass as an exit from the Rishi valley. In either case, the second col at the foot of Changabang should certainly be tried.

## CHAPTER VIII

### INTO THE RISHI VALLEY

I HAVE already mentioned that there was one exception to the fitness and soundness of the Bagini party. Most unfortunately Bruce's knee, which had already been troublesome on the occasion of our descent from Lata Kharak, was now in such a bad state that he was altogether crippled, and as it was impossible to foresee how long he might remain so, he very unselfishly urged Longstaff and me to start at once, leaving him to follow as soon as he was able to do so.

The rest of us, therefore, with Kharbir, Damar Sing and the Three Musketeers, ascended the ridge above Tolma village on May 31, and camped in a coombe on the far side, across which we looked up to the site of our old camp at Lata Kharak. We were accompanied by twenty-three coolies, and a shikari, a sort of satellite of Bhop Chand. Above Tolma we passed a group of the finest deodars I have ever seen, and beyond them a solitary giant, the largest of them all, which measured 41 feet in circumference at a height of 6 feet from the ground.

Next day came the passage of the much-talked-of pass to Darashi. We were up at 5.30, but did not succeed in getting the coolies started till seven. They moved slowly and reluctantly from the very outset, halting frequently, and all talking at once, no doubt with reference to what was in front of them. There was still much snow, and the pass was not yet practicable, according to their view. The three guides

went ahead to make tracks. There were two or three places which must have looked nasty, and in fact were nasty, for loaded men unsuitably shod. An animated conversation took place before the passage of one of these, and I wondered for a moment whether Longstaff, who had a difficult and wearisome job as whipper-in, would be able to get them on. However, they were all assembled on the col at last, after five hours' tedious going. Of course the really dangerous part of the journey was still before us; but this everybody knew, and it was pretty clear that, having come thus far, they had made up their minds to go through with it. The height of the col is 14,700 feet.

About one o'clock the three guides started again to make a road over the *mauvais pas*, while Longstaff boiled a thermometer, and I basked on the other side of the col on a slope of deliciously dry grass ending in a terrific abyss. The first and worst portion of the track could be seen from the col. There was a nearly horizontal traverse rising at the end to cross a narrow ridge jutting out into the void, as it seemed, then a short drop, free from snow, and a similar traverse to another ridge. This process was repeated three or four times altogether. I was the last to leave the col except a sheep and a goat and the man in charge of them. The two animals showed no respect for the situation, and attempted in the most unsuitable places to force a passage between my legs. A block took place at each ridge, and an hour elapsed before I reached the corner where one loses sight of the col. There was a little more traversing after this, but the worst was over, and nothing then remained but a steep, but safe, snow couloir and some rough scrambling.

The scenery was fine, and for a short time included Nanda Devi, but we had already seen it to greater advantage from the peak above Lata Kharak. The really remarkable feature was the view *down* into the chasm of the Rishi, whose waters were actually visible at times, 8000 feet below us. I have certainly never crossed a wilder place.

By 3.30 I was sitting on the little ridge just above Darashi with Alexis, who confided to me that he was *bien heureux* to be there with all the coolies safe, and that he had had great anxiety all day as to whether we should get through. I entirely agreed; there were twenty-five coolies, and a slip on the steps in the snow at almost any part would have meant instant and certain death. The coolies are good men, plucky and sure-footed. When the time came for their return, we were anxious to send a competent person with an ice-axe to see them through. The Brocherels took a very serious view of this matter, and maintained that the passage of the traverses the reverse way, being partly downhill, would be worse than the way in; but all suggestions of help were rejected with derision. They were quite ready to tackle the passage by themselves—without loads. When Bruce followed us in, a little later, he had no difficulty in getting men to come with him; and on our return journey we found that the track, then almost entirely free from snow, was perfectly safe, though not suited, as the guide-books say, to persons subject to giddiness. It was really a question of time, of a week or perhaps ten days. But I strongly advise future travellers who find the season a late one, as we did, in respect to snow, to wait the extra week; there is plenty to do hard by.

In another quarter of an hour we were at Darashi. It is an upland alp or *maidan*, the Dunassau of Graham's narrative, with a rude stone cabin, and other signs of its use as a place of pasturage, lying a good deal lower than the col, but still many thousands of feet above the Rishi chasm, which can be advantageously seen from the crags which jut out from the *maidan*. Longstaff made the height of the camp 13,280 feet; it is close to the spot marked 12,950b on the G.T.S. map. Graham puts it at about 15,800 feet, but does not say how this estimate was obtained.

A gentle slope, which was then still covered with snow, leads up to the ridge bounding the *maidan* on its eastern side. The lowest depression in this ridge is a little over 14,000 feet; it projects southwards far out into the Rishi valley, rising to 14,630 feet. On the other side there is a very abrupt drop to the valley in which Dibrugheta lies (11,730 feet); the highest point falls away in a magnificent and very conspicuous cliff, the "Curtain" of Longstaff's narrative. We got to the ridge on June 2 in a little over half an hour; the caravan went down the steep descent of 2500 feet to the stream at its eastern foot, and so reached Dibrugheta, while I followed the ridge to the north to look for barhal.

It would be an easy walk to the head of the valley, and there is said to be another route over it into the Tolma glen. I went some distance up it, and had a good look at Dunagiri, and another valley which runs up towards Dunagiri, and would, I think, offer a better line for attacking it than the one from the Tolma glen. I failed to get near the barhal, but had three leisurely shots at some very confiding ptarmigan, which had evidently never been fired at before, and succeeded in knocking over two of them.

When I arrived in camp, quite early, I found that Longstaff, having been informed that three shots had

THE RISHI VALLEY.

been heard, promptly had a sheep killed, in order to make it likelier that I had killed a barhal, because if I had, the sheep would not be wanted.

If anybody finds the logic of this proceeding obscure, I cannot help him; it is something—as the schoolboy said when asked to define an axiom—so simple that you cannot explain it.

The camping-ground is a charming spot, a little below the junction of the principal valley with the one which descends from the direction of Dunagiri. Their streams have cut fairly deep ravines, between which spreads a grassy plateau terminating in a steep forest-clad slope which ends, as everything hereabouts does sooner or later, in a precipice overhanging the Rishi river.

It was the sight of this plateau which had delighted the eyes of the Bagini party at the end of their terrific day's coasting along the slopes of the Niti peak on May 25.

I must here begin to refer to Graham's journey. He wrote a very short paper in the *Alpine Journal*, which appeared in August 1884; and a much fuller narrative in *Good Words* (January, February and March 1885). My quotations, except where the contrary is stated, are from the latter. His account of the day's march from Darashi runs as follows: "We swagged all our things up to the ridge, then down to a steep ravine through which a stream was dashing which gave us some trouble to cross. *This stream* [which I take to be the one at the foot of the 2500 feet slope] *is marked on the map as a glacier*, one of those many mistakes which are unpardonable in a survey scale one inch to the mile. Our progress was very slow, partly owing to our having to work double stages, there being fifteen loads for nine of us all told, and partly owing to the nature of the ground, which not only was very broken and precipitous, but quite *terra incognita* to the whole party. We finally camped at a place called Debritigurh, on the southern spur of the range running south from Dunagiri."

It is at this point that he makes his criticism on the work of the surveyors. Now, the statement which I have italicised is a mistake, and the explanation of it is curious. The cardinal error of the G.T.S. map which was described in the last chapter, and is apparent to any one who ascends the heights across the valley between the Trisuli nala and the Rishi, is wholly beyond the ken of a person arriving at Dibrugheta. The map was quite correct so far as Graham's knowledge went, and his attack on its accuracy is premature and unjustified. But, though it sounds paradoxical, the actual error in the map did contribute to his: he believed—no other explanation of his statement is possible—that he was farther on than was really the case, and that he had reached the erroneously represented upper portion of the valley which coincides at its mouth with the true Arhamani valley. It was an intelligible mistake, but I do not think he could have made it if the latter had been correctly shown.

Graham gives a vivid description of the next stage of his journey. "Occasionally we had to hang on by a tuft of grass or a bunch of Alpine roses, and I do not exaggerate when I say that for half the total day's work, handhold was as necessary as foothold. By nightfall, after twelve hours' work, we had gained some three miles in absolute distance, and this, perhaps better than anything, will give an idea of the labour involved in working along these slopes. We camped on a little space, the only one we could find, which was not quite so steep as the rest. . . ." There they halted for a day, and then descended to the river, which they were unable to cross owing to the unusual volume of water; they camped there, and Graham and Emil Boss proceeded up the right bank of the stream to the mouth of the Rishi cleft. Being unable to force their way up it they returned to the camp by the river, where they found Kaufmann and the shikari; the coolies had all bolted, so they "abandoned everything that was not absolutely necessary, and managed, in a couple of days, to swag back to Debritigurh."

It is difficult to make out at what point Graham reached the Rishi; and Longstaff is inclined to believe that he never got to it at all, and that the stream which he arrived at was the Arhamani. This is quite possible; it is certainly odd that he makes no mention of coming upon the Arhamani stream in the course of his exploration of the Rishi cleft.

Our coolies left Dibrugheta at about half-past six. There were several *mauvais pas*, at some of which I was not too proud to accept a helping hand; but our rate of progress compared with Graham's is a good example of the extent to which time is invariably and inevitably wasted in crossing quite unknown country. The shikari, and probably some of the other men also, had been over the ground more than once, and knew exactly the right way, which was not always the obvious one, and we were all down by the river by eleven o'clock.

It was grey and discoloured, more like a Swiss glacier stream than most of the Himalayan torrents, and almost bridged by some huge boulders. The place is known as Duti, and there is a little bit of level ground a short distance below the boulder bridge, just big enough to pitch the camp upon. The coolies, of course, wanted us to camp there, and protested that they could or would go no farther, so a palaver took place between Longstaff, the shikari, and some representative coolies. Longstaff, who was impatient to reach the Trisuli nala without delay, offered them two days' pay if they would finish the march at once; if not they must come on the next day, and only receive the same amount. He made a diplomatic display of indifference as to which way they decided, and after a little talking it over amongst themselves they decided that if they might stop long enough to cook a meal and eat it, they would come on.

All this took place on the far side of the torrent: we heard later that the men had been inclined, on their first arrival at the river bank, to refuse to cross. One man took the lead and said he would leave his load and go back rather than do so, whereupon Kharbir very artfully promised to make things unpleasant for him alone, "because you are the first; I don't care what the others may do." This was more than the man had bargained for; he crossed, and the others followed. Once they were over, the battle was half won.

NANDA DEVI.

We scrambled for an hour or more to the top of a thickly-wooded bluff which fell precipitously into the Rishi, and there in front of us, framed in the narrow cleft which starts from its very base, was Nandi Devi. I photographed it amidst a thick crowd of coolies, who grinned delightedly when I pulled out the legs of the tripod, and again when they were pushed back into their place. Then making a half-right turn, we descended, still scrambling through thick woods and undergrowth, into the Trisuli nala, where a fair camping ground was found soon after three o'clock.

Before proceeding to the narrative of our two assaults on Trisul, I will complete what I have to say with regard to Graham's two subsequent ascents from theRishi valley. We left him at Dibrugheta; where as soon as they got back the weather changed, "and we had four most perfect days for climbing" (*Alpine Journal*). Of this climbing he gives in *Good Words* a fairly detailed account. They sent back the shikari to fetch some more coolies from Tolma. He "vowed to bring them back in three days." This matter disposed of, "we started to ascend a very noble peak, nameless unfortunately, and only known by a number (A 21), as if it were a convict. The peak is south-east of Dunagiri, and is of a very curious shape, but one fairly common in the Himalayas. It is built just like a wedge with a level top, perhaps a quarter of a mile long, whilst the eastern and western sides are slopes of 60 to 70 and of course utterly inaccessible. During the ascent to our sleeping-place, some 18,000 feet above the sea, we put up a great many of the beautiful snow-pheasant called 'monal' in India, and Impeyan pheasant in England; so many were there that we called our peak Mount Monal." Unfortunately, no other details are given with regard to this day's journey, and there is no clue to the position of the sleeping-place, on which everything hinges. Neither can one say how he arrived at his estimate of its height. I imagine it to have been the result of a calculation based on the height of the peak he climbed from it, which he assumed to be 22,516 feet. It will be remembered that he greatly overrated the height of Darashi.

On the second day, according to the brief account in the *Alpine Journal*, they "achieved the ascent very successfully from the western ridge. It was a fair climb but presented no great difficulties." The fuller narrative in *Good Words* continues as follows: "The ascent from the south-eastern arête presented no difficulties, and we reached the top, 22,516 feet, again with perfect freedom from any unusual distress. This was the highest ascent on record up to date, though we ourselves passed it by some 1500 feet when we ascended Kabru some ten weeks later. Almost due east lay yet a third peak (A 22), one of the very finest aiguilles I have ever seen. I could not suppose it to be possible, but as it was the only one within reach, I thought we might at least have a try. We accordingly swagged up our things, meaning to sleep in a cavern whose mouth we saw some 4000 feet above us; we reached its mouth, and Boss entered to explore";

(4000 feet must be a misprint for 1000 or 400 feet, probably the latter). The cavern was full of ice, "a true subterranean glacier," and they had to lie down outside it in their sleeping-bags.

On the third day they started, after a very cold night, to attack the aiguille. "About 800 feet of steep, loose moraine was passed and then we reached the top of the arête, and immediately the peak stood before us, rising more than 2000 feet above, with not a line or trace of snow." They crossed the face to the eastern arête, which they reached in three hours and proceeded to ascend, but after some difficult climbing they were defeated, and returned to Dibrugheta, where they finished their provisions, as they "expected the shikari to turn up every minute."

Next morning Kaufmann returned to their "last stage" to fetch some abandoned meat tins, Graham went off after monal, while Boss went forward to find the shepherds at Darashi. Boss rejoined them late in the evening with the shikari. "The stream which flowed from the Dunagiri glacier had risen so much that it was above Boss's waist, and much too strong for the little hillmen." In the morning, however, they were able to cross early, and came on to the camp. The party then started "on the back trail," and were back in Naini Tal on August 12.

I have tried in vain to work out Graham's itinerary in full. He is very chary of dates, giving none after his first arrival at Darashi, and there are serious discrepancies between those given in the *Alpine Journal* and in *Good Words*. However, the succession of events during the important period is sufficiently clear, and we now come to the question, What were his two peaks, Mount Monal and the aiguille? I confess that I have been entirely unable to arrive at any satisfactory conclusions with regard to them except in a negative sense.

The first reference to them occurs in the account of the attempt on Dunagiri. Graham and Boss had been enveloped in mist, and were thinking of turning back, when there was a sudden brief break, and, he continues in the account in the *Alpine Journal*, "we instantly saw the great height that we had reached. Actually below us lay a splendid peak A 21, to which we afterwards gave the name of Mount Monal, 22,516. Over its very summit we saw A 22, 21,001, the remaining peak of the Dunagiri chain. We cannot, therefore, have been less than 22,700 feet, and the summit, not 500 feet above us, was in full sight." The parallel passage in *Good Words* is as follows: "Right above us were some black rocks which we knew formed the top, whilst towards the south-east a splendid peak, A 21 which is by the Trigonometrical Survey 22,516 feet, lay well below us, as we were able to see a third peak, which is 21,001 feet, over its summit. We were at the elevation of 22,700 feet, and the summit looked quite close." Whether he actually attained a height of 22,700 feet on Dunagiri is not a matter of any particular moment, but it seems to me to be clear that his estimate was entirely based on the assumption that the mountain whose summit he saw "well below" him was A 21, and that it was only as an inference from this that he "knew" the black rocks above him formed the top.

This passage in *Good Words* is, perhaps, a shade less emphatic, but substantially the same as the one in the *Alpine Journal*, except that the words "the remaining peak of the Dunagiri chain" are dropped. The same omission occurs again later; when he comes to visit these two peaks, he again in the very condensed account in the *Alpine Journal* speaks of the latter as "the third and last peak in the Dunagiri range," his A 21 being presumably the second, while nothing of the sort appears in the more detailed narrative in *Good Words*.

I find it very difficult to believe that such a description of the true A 21 could occur to any one seeing it, however briefly and imperfectly, from high up on Dunagiri: it is separated from Dunagiri by the whole of the long low-lying ridge that forms the southern boundary of the Bagini glacier, and is the first of the entirely distinct mass of mountains which compose its great eastern wall. However, it is unnecessary here to lay any stress on this point: the really conclusive fact is that Changabang, or A 21, cannot be much, if at all, less than three miles distant from Dunagiri as the crow flies, and that Graham could not possibly have seen an adjacent peak of 21,001 feet over the top of it from a height of 22,700 feet, if such a peak had been there to see. But the peak on the far side of Changabang is Kalanka (A 21a), a massive snowy mountain, 22,735 feet in height; nothing more unlike Graham's aiguille could be imagined.

These considerations alone seem to me to settle completely the question of the identity of Changabang with Mount Monal. An examination of Graham's narrative of his climbs leads independently, and no less decisively, to the same conclusion.

To any one who has taken the trouble to master the topography of the region under discussion as set forth in the preceding chapter, it will be apparent that to reach Changabang from Dibrugheta, Graham must in the first place have got to the head of the Arhamani glacier, and it will be remembered that the Bagini party took the best part of two days to cover the same distance in the reverse direction. But he would still have been a long way from the south-eastern arête of Changabang. In order to reach it he must have crossed into the Nanda Devi basin by the route which I have referred to as probably the best one for that purpose on p. 94. Could any party, however speedy, have covered this ground, without any previous knowledge of it, ascended and descended Changabang, spent several hours on another peak, and returned to Dibrugheta in the course of three days? To me the question seems to be outside the range of reasonable discussion.

The principal argument in favour of the correctness of Graham's identification of his two peaks—apart from the one which may be concisely stated in the form "He said so, and he ought to know"—is the extreme difficulty of suggesting any plausible alternatives.

One possible candidate for the place of Mount Monal is the snowy peak above the Arhamani valley which is seen in the illustration facing p. 126. It answers rather well to the description of a wedge-shaped peak (I can see nothing wedge-like about Changabang from any point of view), and, moreover, in a *very* rough sketch which I made on June 18 on the back of a map, there is dimly discoverable beyond it something which I certainly must have intended for such an aiguille as Graham describes. These are the points in its favour: against it are, first, the fact that these peaks cannot in any sense be reckoned as part of the Dunagiri chain; and secondly, difficulties of time and distance, which are considerable, though not so overwhelming as in the case of Changabang.

And connected with these is a difficulty of a less tangible kind to which I cannot help attaching a good deal of weight. He had just returned from the head of the valley, and it had taken him two days' hard scrambling to get there and two days more to get back. I find it very hard to believe that he started again in the same direction with the intention of making an expedition which would involve a journey equally far in the same direction, and actually covered the distance in less than half the time, without making any topographical comments or any reference to his previous journey. Considerations of this kind point to the conclusion that any one relying solely on Graham's own descriptions, and unhampered by any references to peaks marked on the map, would start to look for his 18,000 feet sleeping-place and his subterranean glacier somewhere high up on the spur of Dunagiri, which terminates in Niti peak No. 8, 17,056 feet. There alone some summit might be found which could be regarded as part of the Dunagiri chain, and which Graham might have seen actually below him, from Dunagiri itself. But I admit that any such summit would be a miserably inadequate substitute for A 21, though, on the other hand, it must be borne in mind that Graham himself dismisses his successful ascent of Mount Monal with an off-hand brevity which is almost contemptuous. And there I must leave the subject. I am afraid I have already treated it at inordinate length.

The RISHI RIVER at Duti.

## CHAPTER IX

### THE FIRST ATTEMPT ON TRISUL

LONGSTAFF declared that the Brocherels wanted to start for Trisul the next day. It is a remarkable fact that, sooner or later, every one in our company said to me of every other member of it that he was in too great a hurry; and I was able to agree impartially and sincerely nearly every time; but I think, on this occasion, it was a libel, on Alexis at all events. The following day was the 4th June, and we both knew what a *non dies* was; but when morning came Longstaff was off after barhal, and it was Alexis who stayed to enjoy a *jour de repos*, and shake his head over the shooting expedition, and the regrettable fact that Monsieur Longstaff was *trop vif*.

The camp (about 11,600 feet) was a confined and unattractive spot; the sun was off it early and reached it late, though I have a vivid recollection of a really astonishing light-effect which was produced when it did appear above the hilltops, and shot its rays down through the birch trees: the tattered strips of bark became transparent, almost dazzling, and shone like yellow and copper flames.

High up on the other side of the Rishi could be seen the place where the Bagini party had camped on May 24, but very little of our own valley was visible.

On the 5th we started at 7.15, and after struggling for nearly an hour through a tangle of pine, birch, and rhododendron, emerged into the open; a short distance in front of us a large glacier, descending from the right, extended right across the valley; Longstaff had reached it rather higher up on the previous day. Soon after half-past ten we were on the far side of it, and looking down into a broad open expanse of grass with the stream from the Trisul glacier flowing through it, and plenty of scrub for fuel. It was the one place in the valley clearly designed by nature for a camping-ground. The temptation to stop there was irresistible, and early as it was, we decided without much hesitation to do so. The scrub which abounded suggested the name of "Juniper Camp." Had we known of the place before, our obvious course would have been to halt at Duti on June 3, and bring the whole camp on to it before dismissing the coolies.

The glacier we had just crossed, for which we were given the name of "Beta Toli," descends in a fine ice-fall from the neighbourhood of point 20,842 feet, which figures so conspicuously in the view from the peak near Lata Kharak. It comes right up against the cliffs on the east, and the Trisul stream finds its way through by a tunnel under the ice. We were camping at a height of about 12,650 feet, some hundreds of feet lower than the Trisul glacier, the dirty snout of which only was visible, in the jaws of a narrow defile.

The next day, June 6, we started at six o'clock, and in about two hours were on the left-hand moraine of the Trisul glacier, with the way lying clear for several miles ahead. The great glaciers of Garhwal are all admirable highways; they rise regularly and gently, and provide far the best going in the whole country; where the surface is broken, or, as more often happens, thickly piled up with huge boulders, there is generally a fair path along a moraine, and here there was an excellent one.

We were in a huge trough, and the surrounding scenery, though impressive from the mere size and scale of things, was, on the whole, monotonous. On the east the great rampart which shut us off from the Nanda Devi basin rose steadily, its craggy cliffs giving place by degrees to steep snow faces of unbroken whiteness which merged in those of the main Trisul ridge. The cliffs on the west (our right hand) were much lower, and came to an end in a low bluff, some distance beyond which the glacier made a great sweep round towards Trisul. On the map it looked a long way to the corner, but we had hoped in the absence of serious obstacles to reach it in the course of the day. It was now apparent that there were no obstacles whatever, and that we should get round it comfortably; so we plodded on in very leisurely fashion, sometimes on the moraine, sometimes on beds of snow to the right of it, every one going his own pace. Dunagiri rose up finely behind us, and some barhal appeared on the skyline on the right; but it was a dull trudge.

The bluff was reached at about half-past one, and

the moraine, which curved round and upwards, was followed for another three-quarters of an hour, till we were well round the corner. Here we came to a halt, being now some hundreds of feet above the glacier, which swept on towards the base of Trisul, apparently at a dead level. The moraine provided a very fair camping-place, and it would be perfectly feasible to bring coolies to it, and send them back the same day to "Juniper Camp." The line of cliffs, now quite low, continued round the corner, and shut us in on the north. Westward, too, the skyline was low, steep stony slopes, to-morrow's route, and fine ice-cliffs, overhanging a belt of black rocks. Above these lay quite unknown ground. Far away in the background appeared what looked like a snow peak, but it was really only a fold in the great ridge leading to Trisul. East and south we looked across the Trisul glacier, buried deeply beneath a thick carpet of snow, at its boundary walls rising to 22,000 feet or more, the whole forming one continuous expanse of unrelieved white. Though there was no snow in our immediate neighbourhood, the effect was so dazzling that most of us kept on our spectacles till sunset.

Dinner that evening consisted of cocoa, which was supremely "grateful and comforting," biscuits and jam, followed after an interval of twenty minutes by a cup of "maggi" soup, mixed with plasmon powder almost to the consistency of paste; this was to me the most sustaining, digestible, and generally satisfactory kind of food that our resources produced; but for some reason it was never repeated. I did not sleep much, and was somewhat troubled by difficulty in breathing, but felt cheerful and sanguine.

We breakfasted on June 7 mainly on cocoa which had been brewed overnight, and kept warm in thermos bottles : it was excellent, and there was only one fault to find with it—that there was not more of it. A start was made at 5.25, and a scrambling climb of an hour and a quarter brought us to a plateau on a level with the top of the ice-cliffs. A further ascent of twenty minutes, and we were on the edge of a broad undulating snowy plateau which led us gently up to the ridge that forms the watershed between the Trisuli nala and the Nandakganga.

Over this plateau we plodded laboriously with brief halts at intervals that tended to get shorter and shorter. My general recollection of the walk is that Henri and Alexis were always sitting down two or three hundred yards ahead ; very slowly one arrived there too, and had hardly joined them before they were off again, striding away in the distance, and the endless process of overhauling them began again. At length we approached the other side of the plateau, under steep slopes with a small dip or col, which had been staring us in the face for hours, and never seemed to get any nearer. At 12.30 some rocks not very far from the foot of these slopes just below the col suggested tiffin, but it was not partaken of with the usual enthusiasm. We pushed on up easier slopes to the left, where the ridge broadened out into the rounded fold which we had seen from the camp on the previous evening. This was the limit of what I have seen of this side of Trisul ;

the Brocherels halted rather unexpectedly at about a quarter-past two, and proceeded to unpack the tents and pitch them in the snow, when we had reached a point not quite on a level with the little col. The place sloped considerably; there was no shelter of any kind, and the tents were hardly up when the wind began to blow pretty hard, with occasional showers of fine powdery dry snow. The wind was so penetrating that the primus stove could not be got to work, and it was soon clear that there would be no "maggi" and plasmon that night. Though we were an hour to the good, we should have been in all other respects much better off at the place where we had tiffined, which was level, and enjoyed a certain amount of protection from the wind. However, there we were, and there was nothing for it but to make the best of it, *i.e.* to get snug in one's tent before sundown; so Inderbinen and I retreated to ours with a tin of biscuits, two large bags of candied fruits and raisins, and a thermos bottle of melted snow.

The height of this camp has since worked out at just over 20,000 feet, the highest elevation I have ever reached. Though I was travelling more lightly than any one else, my load was substantially heavier than any that I have ever carried in the Alps; but, after making due allowance for this, it was undeniably a very much greater grind than it would have been at a lower level. At the same time I had felt quite ready to go on at the same pace for another couple of hours, and but for a very slight headache, which soon left me, was reasonably well and comfortable.

I managed to get a little sleep, but the difficulty about that had nothing to do with altitude. The wind raged round the tents as if it had never had tents to play with before: one heard voices muttering through it, much as one sometimes hears them through the sound of running water, as though the storm demons were debating what to do next. Then would come a short lull, followed by a flap or two, and then a violent bang against the bottom of the canvas, just as if a gigantic fist was punching snow underneath the tent. It was a rather weird experience, and boring and annoying, but nothing more than that. The dread of cold nights at great altitudes had been my bugbear ever since the journey began; but I did not suffer from cold, and have spent many far more uncomfortable nights in the Alps and elsewhere.

Inderbinen was in a much worse plight: he had had a bad headache, and had been unable to eat when we arrived; all night through he had suffered severely from headache, sickness, and difficulty in breathing, and in the morning he was still sick and miserable, with no appetite, but a raging thirst, which there was very little means of satisfying. I thought this was an excellent opportunity of testing the pneumatogen cartridges, and tried to show him how to inhale; but it only made him sneeze, and, after one or two half-hearted efforts, "I suppose that will be enough, sir," he said lugubriously. I swallowed a violent desire to laugh, and gave it up.

It must have been nearly nine o'clock when I first peeped out; everything was quiet and motionless in the other tents, so I retired for an hour, and then had another look. The Brocherels were just coming in from a short reconnaissance, and every one emerged to discuss the situation. The tents looked forlorn and dishevelled, and the place well deserved its name of "Misery Camp." Longstaff had decided to send down the Three Musketeers, who had not been particularly

happy during the night, and to stop where we were and try to reach Trisul to-morrow if the weather improved. It was clear that Inderbinen must go back with the Gurkhas, and I was more than half-inclined to do so too, partly because I did not believe there was any chance of the weather improving, and partly because I did not exactly see where I was to spend the night.

Longstaff invited me to join him and Kharbir, saying cheerfully that there was lots of room. A glance into their tent assured me that this statement was unduly optimistic—in fact, that there was no room at all. However, it appeared that there would be accommodation for Inderbinen down below, and eventually I elected to stay, and our tent, which had been taken down, was put up again. In a short time Inderbinen and the Gurkhas had vanished, the rest of us were once more under cover, and communication became rare, for the storm was still raging, and every visit to the outer world meant a considerable increase to the amount of snow inside. The last palaver took place, during a short spell of sunshine and quiet, about mid-day, and at 12.30 Longstaff solemnly bade me "Good-night."

It was not long afterwards that I discovered that my tin of biscuits had disappeared, but by that time it was again snowing and blowing hard, and I was not keen enough about food to go out on a voyage of discovery. In the interests of science I tried whether a dose from the pneumatogen cartridge would assist me to enjoy a pipe. I think it certainly did; and I found I could smoke with satisfaction for several minutes continuously, which I had not been able to do before inhaling the oxygen; even so, however, it left me rather breathless. The sun shone brilliantly at intervals, but sharp showers of fine hard snow continued to fall, and appeared to grow longer and more violent as the afternoon wore slowly on. I lay and wondered whether the toes which had suffered on the Bagini glacier would recover circulation before nightfall. Luckily they did so, and I got through the night, which in its general character was a repetition of the preceding one, pretty well; indeed, I afterwards found to my surprise that I had been less inconvenienced by the cold than any one else. Occasionally, when the wind was specially violent, I was seized with a panic of fear that the tent ropes might give way; but the idea was very ill founded: the pegs were immovably frozen, and next morning, as Longstaff put it, "we literally tore ourselves up by the roots." There was no question of anything but retreat.

I was so weak with hunger that I could scarcely crawl as far as the camping-place on the moraine, and to my consternation there was no one there. I should have sat down and cried if I had not espied Longstaff's rucksack; the others had gone to fetch water, and a few minutes later I was revived by swallowing a whole tin of sardines, and several plasmon biscuits, and also enjoyed a big drink, though I had not been consciously thirsty up till that time.

After a long halt (for the place was sheltered, and the sun had come out) we made a *cache* of some of the provisions, and set off again. The whole descent from "Misery Camp" to "Juniper Camp" occupied four to four and a half hours' walking. It is one of the minor compensations of high altitudes that going downhill is not more laborious than usual, and consequently descents are always accomplished with unexpected ease and rapidity.

We found the Three Musketeers ready for us, and

Damar Sing well advanced with his plane-table sheets; but there was still no news of Bruce; and I think it was the consequent uncertainty as to when our store of provisions would be replenished which caused a certain parsimony to prevail in the use of biscuits, etc. Dinner that night consisted of barhal soup, chunks of fried barhal meat, and three gingerbread biscuits apiece; and on the following day, too, we subsisted on an almost exclusively meat diet, which seemed to agree admirably with Longstaff and the Brocherels, but certainly did not agree with me.

Snow drove us early to bed, and the night of June 9th-10th was extremely cold; next morning the rivulet which flowed past the camp was frozen hard; and where yesterday little cascades had trickled down the face of the eastern wall of the valley, the dark cliffs were now streaked with frosted white ribands. Longstaff was grimly determined to make another start on the 11th, come what might; my views on the question vacillated throughout the day with the changes of the weather: during one or two short spells of sunshine and warmth I thought I might possibly go too, but snow and cold prevailed, and by the evening I was so thoroughly out of sorts that I had to abandon the idea finally. A lingering hope remained that something catastrophic in the way of a snowstorm might compel the others to wait for twenty-four hours, but at 6 A.M. on the 11th Longstaff, the Brocherels, and Kharbir set off undaunted, though not very sanguine, amidst most unpromising weather-signs, with Dhan Lal and Buddhi Chand as porters. Kharbir was seriously advised to stay behind on account of his toes, which had not yet recovered from their frost-bite, but he entirely declined even to discuss the question.

I crept gloomily into the tent vacated by the Gurkhas, and was taken charge of by Kul Bahadur and a coolie whose name has vanished, but whom I remember gratefully as "the man in the black coat." A few hours later I rejoined Inderbinen, who was also rather down on his luck, at the lower camp, and presently found myself involved in a long conversation with Kul Bahadur and the shikari. I believed, but with no great confidence, that we had been discussing the state of the larder, and that I had given them permission to kill a sheep; a view which was confirmed later by the appearance of the sheep's kidneys (admirably cooked by Kul Bahadur) for dinner.

We amused ourselves on the 12th by climbing in about two hours—some of it was a real climb—to a crag opposite the camp, from which we could see right up the Rishi cleft. It was a most impressive spectacle, though only the extreme end of the north-western arête of Nanda Devi was visible, the main mass of the mountain being round the corner to the right. A passage up the bottom of the ravine appeared to be very unpromising, and it seemed to me that a traverse of the cliffs on either side, if possible at all, would be fearfully long and difficult, and quite impracticable for a party attempting to get into the Nanda Devi basin with stores and tents. Close by a fine view was obtained of the Arhamani glacier, and of Changabang, which, seen end on, presented itself as a tall slender

THE ARHAMANI AND RISHI GORGES.

cone of extreme steepness; its curious colouring made it look strangely pale and unsubstantial, a mere ghost of a mountain.

Nothing was to be gained by going farther, so I took some photographs and returned, thinking much of our scattered band: Bruce, of whom we had had no news; and the Trisul party, who I imagined would now be camping 1000 feet or so above our "Misery Camp." It was beautifully fine, but there were signs that up aloft a strong wind was blowing.

On the 18th I went up the slopes behind the camp, armed to the teeth with gun, rifle, and camera, visiting much the same ground that Longstaff had been over on June 4, but I only succeeded in bagging one ptarmigan, sitting (or, to be strictly accurate, walking), and a very poor lot of photographs. They were the only ones taken with this camera on *plates*, which were not at least fairly successful.

It was unfortunate that I had not chosen this walk the day before. The view from about 3000 feet above the camp, extending from the head of the Trisul valley to the Bagini pass, and including Nanda Devi and the north-eastern arm of the Nanda Devi basin, was extraordinarily fine; but the day was cloudy and overcast, and my hopes for the Trisul party sank low.

Returning down the valley, I was aware of new faces and some additional tents, and to my surprise and delight found Bruce lying in one of them, weak and feverish, but overflowing with conversation and in excellent spirits.

The trouble in his knee had finally revealed itself as

an abscess. He had dealt with it in a masterful and drastic fashion, and immediately afterwards, utterly regardless of his state of health, had left Surai Thota with two more Gurkhas and as many coolies as were available, having given orders for some more coolies to meet us at Dibrugheta on the 17th with a fresh supply of provisions. On the 11th he had been prostrated at Dibrugheta by an attack of fever, and after remaining there for a day had struggled on to Duti, and finally here.

He had scarcely made all this clear when another surprise followed. In walked Alexis Brocherel, his face skinned and swollen almost beyond recognition, but as imperturbable as usual, and tranquilly gave us his news. The dauntless four had reached the summit of Trisul the previous day!

## CHAPTER X

### THE ASCENT OF TRISUL

In accordance with what had been originally contemplated they had gone up, beyond the moraine, and camped at about 17,450 feet on the rocks to the right of and above the ice-cliffs which rose above our old moraine camp; but from there Longstaff had resolved to try and reach the summit in a day, and not to tempt the wind again on the exposed snow-slopes higher up. Details came thick and fast as we sat at dinner, a very cheery party, happy to be once more reunited. The two points which impressed me most at the time were that it had been a really terrific grind, of which the mere description filled me with dismay, and that the bitter wind had been a friend in disguise, and had very much diminished the difficulty of breathing during the ascent. But I must leave Longstaff to tell his own story.

"Snow continued to fall till the early hours. We tried to start (June 12) at 4 A.M., but I could not face the cold, which attacked my feet and hands before I could get my frozen boots on, although I had kept the latter inside my sleeping bag all night. However, we started at 5.30 A.M., and as we carried only the very lightest loads we made rapid progress. We reached our old upper camp (20,050 feet) by 10 A.M., where we remained half an hour to eat a small meal of raisins and plasmon biscuits, for we had all fully realised that it was most unwise for us to try to negotiate a heavy

meal at such an altitude. Seeing signs of crevasses ahead we put on the rope, Alexis leading, then Kharbir, Henri and myself. Then on we went up the snow-slopes, of continuous steepness but withal quite easy, in a S.W. by S. direction. My breathing was very rapid, and I felt very feeble, but I was securely tied on to the rope and could not escape. The *tourmentes* of wind-driven snow, to which this slope of the mountain seems very liable, were at times almost paralysing in their intensity, yet I am sure that we bore the cold better than we should have borne extreme heat. At noon we found we had reached 21,000 feet, and here Alexis had to take off the small snow-shoes (racquettes) with

which he had been breaking a track through the crust of new snow, as the slope became too steep for their use. I began to doubt my capacity for maintaining the pace much longer, but Alexis and Kharbir seemed quite happy, and Henri offered to pull on my rope as much as I liked, so I pocketed my pride and consented to this breach of the rules. Except for the briefest halts to recover breath, we now rose rapidly and continuously, the slopes being at that particular angle of steepness which enables the climber to make height most rapidly, and all the peaks in sight sank below us except Nanda Devi. As we neared the summit the bitter west wind again swooped down on us, rattling the icicles on our beards and moustaches, and half-smothering us in whirling snow. Suddenly the slope ended, and Alexis turned and shouted to me. We found ourselves standing on a flat-topped dome of snow, which forms the apex of the huge triangular snow-field set at a steep angle upon the north-east face of the mountain, and along the western edge of which we had climbed; the guides hailed it as the summit, and Henri planted the stick and square of canvas he had insisted on bringing up. But I was not yet satisfied, for just beyond us, across a dip in the ridge, was a most provoking cornice, which seemed to be a few feet higher and cut off the view to the south. I do not think I am exaggerating when I say that it was only by the exercise of considerable mental resolution that I had been able to turn myself into a sufficiently mechanical machine to keep up the pace so far, and I was naturally extremely fatigued; but now excitement made me lose all sense of it. There was some demur to going farther so late in the day—it was 4 P.M.—and, as I could not make myself heard above the gale, I took the lead and pushed on. Not knowing the size of the cornice, I had to keep well down on its western slope. The snow was frozen hard, and, as I was the only one wearing crampons, I soon received orders to cut steps; I did not notice

NANDA DEVI FROM THE SUMMIT OF TRISUL.

any difficulty in doing so, but the distance was very short, and I soon crawled on to the cornice and looked over the edge down the astounding southern precipice of Trisul, a sheer drop of over 6000 feet. I remember no feeling of elation at having accomplished the ascent —I suppose I was too tired for that—but on looking round me, I realised, as I have seldom done before, that higher reward which carries us year after year, through toil and discomfort, back to the mountains. Remote from the world, the sense of isolation was complete; the inhabited earth was at our feet, but we stood on a different planet, removed from it by undreamed-of spaces; and the turmoil of the elements around us intensified the indescribable majesty of that stupendous vision. Over the foothills to the south was piled a dense copper-coloured haze—a dust-storm from the plains—but to the west I seemed to be gazing into space itself across the scarp of the Himalaya, whose lines fell in long sweeping curves to the vast unbroken plains, lapping at their feet as did the ocean of a forgotten epoch.

"The cold was very trying, and turning back almost at once we regained the first summit, which proved to be highest after all. It was 4.30 P.M. before we began the descent. I felt quite done up, but had no difficulty with my breathing as soon as I began to go downhill. Going very fast we reached our camp under the cliffs at 7 P.M.; but perhaps my watch was fast, for it was so light that the men insisted on rolling up the tents and sleeping bags, and carried everything down to our old camp on the moraine at 16,500 feet. That night my only desire was for sleep; I was neither hungry nor thirsty, though I had taken very little all day.

"I hope I have made it clear that the two Brocherels, without whose support, moral and physical, I do not think I should have reached the summit, and Kharbir showed no signs of distress during the climb. We ascended from a camp at 17,450 feet to the summit, 23,406 feet—that is to say, 6000 feet in ten hours—the descent of nearly 7000 feet being made in a little over three hours.

"Graham estimated his highest camp on Kabru at 18,500 feet, and reached the summit, 24,000 feet—an ascent of 5500 feet—in a little over nine hours. In each case this gives a rate of approximately 600 feet an hour. Turning to the Alps, the best instance I can remember for comparison is the ascent of Mont Blanc, 15,781 feet, from the Dome Hut, 10,499 feet, on the Italian side. I have twice performed the ascent of 5282 feet in five and a half hours, which gives a rate of 960 feet an hour. In addition to this diminution of progress, I am distinctly conscious of both mental and physical lassitude at very great altitudes; but I have now been to 20,000 feet and over on about ten occasions, and slept at least three, and probably five nights at such altitudes, and my experience confirms me in the belief that the effect of low atmospheric pressure depends on the strength and condition of the climber much more than on the actual altitude he attains. I also believe that the idea of acclimatisation to low pressure is fallacious, for in my experience the effects are cumulative; and it was this consideration which finally determined me to rush the peak from a comparatively low camp."[1]

Beyond the moraine camp, where the party stopped on their descent, the Trisul glacier curves round to the west, running up to the base of Trisul just as the glacier below the Bagini pass sweeps round to the base of Dunagiri. Longstaff and Alexis Brocherel went up the Trisul glacier for one and a half hours on the morning of June 18, and inspected the gap, which he named the Trisul Gap, in the great ridge running eastward from the middle peak of Trisul; it may be regarded as corresponding to the much longer depression between Dunagiri and Changabang. This detour, which enabled Longstaff to lay down correctly the water-parting at this point between the Rishi and the Pindar, was a characteristic display of his thorough-going energy, which never succumbed for a moment to the relaxing influence of unusual elevations. But with regard to another instance of it, the rushing policy described in the last paragraph quoted above, I remain unconvinced, and seem to discern in it considerable traces of that Spartan element in his mountaineering habit of mind which has already been occasionally referred to.

There are arguments for and against such a policy applicable to mountaineering at any level, to say nothing of considerations of pleasure and leisure, but I am here referring to the specific grounds taken up by him. Without venturing to dispute the general proposition as to the cumulative effects of low pressures—a

[1] *Alpine Journal*, vol. xxiv. p. 118.

point on which he speaks with unequalled authority—I believe that where it is a question between two and three days, those effects are more than counterbalanced by the diminution in the amount of effort required on the final day. To put the matter from a personal standpoint, I think I might have reached the top of Trisul on June 8; I cannot flatter myself that I should have got anywhere near it on June 12. In other words, the rushing method is magnificent, but in my humble opinion it is not good strategy.

A magnificent effort it certainly was; and well deserving of the recognition it received at the hands of the Geographical Society in the award of the Gill Memorial, and the cordial congratulations with which it was acclaimed by the Alpine Club at home. As for the congratulations which greeted him when he rejoined us at the foot of the mountain, they were cordial indeed, and something more. Blended with our pleasure in his success was a feeling—almost of relief—that the expedition had undeniably justified itself, and achieved something well worth the doing, whether or not it had established anything in the nature of a "record."

It is impossible here to keep away from the subject of records. Longstaff detests them, so I feel bound to say here—what he has firmly declined to say himself—that the summit of Trisul was then the highest point on the earth's surface which had been reached by man beyond all doubt or controversy, and it still remains the highest mountain in the world of which the complete ascent is undisputed.

## THE ASCENT OF TRISUL

The first undoubted altitude record was established by the Schlagintweit brothers;[1] and it remained unapproached till the time of the Great Trigonometrical Survey of India, in the course of which equal or greater elevations were reached on more than one occasion. In 1874 one of the G.T.S. officers, Mr. I. S. Pococke, attained a height of over 22,000 feet somewhere in the upper Mana valley in Garhwal, but no particulars as to the locality where this feat was accomplished are forthcoming. But the interest in this connection centres mainly round the doings of Mr. W. H. Johnson, who admittedly reached 22,300 feet or thereabouts in 1864; in the following year he visited the Kuen Luen mountains, and reported that he climbed three peaks there, the height of one of which had been fixed three years before at 23,890 feet. This statement was received by his superiors with incredulity; the official view was that either his measurements were wrong or he had mistaken his mountain. The story of his "suppressed ascent" is a very curious one, but too long to be told here. The facts were unearthed by Mr. Freshfield at the time of the controversy with regard to Graham's ascent of Kabru: quite recently Longstaff has gone still more fully into the matter, and brought forward cogent reasons for thinking that the ascent was actually made as alleged.[2] Johnson, it should be added, was an ardent mountaineer, and endeavoured to start a Himalayan Alpine Club, but he received no support and nothing came of the attempt.

[1] See above, p. 22.

[2] *Alpine Journal*, vol. xii. p. 58; vol. xxiv. p. 133.

In an article in *Nature*, on an ascent by M. Wiener of Illimani in the Bolivian Andes in 1877, it is stated that if the estimate of its altitude at 21,224 feet be correct, "M. Wiener has, we believe, not only made the highest ascent which has been made in the Andes, but has attained a greater altitude than has hitherto been reached on the earth out of Asia, and in Asia has only been beaten by Mr. Johnson, who some years ago got to a height of 22,300 feet in Kashmir."[1] The writer, it will be observed, overlooks the Schlagintweits' climb, and ignores, as Graham does, Johnson's alleged ascent in the Kuen Luen range. This is the earliest passage that I have come across in which the question of "the world's record for altitude" is explicitly raised, but since 1883, when Graham did or did not get up Kabru, it has excited more or less continuous interest.

Sir Martin Conway drew attention to the fact that the climbers of Pioneer Peak had accomplished the highest undisputed ascent yet made,[2] and a few years later he congratulated Mr. S. M. Vines on having established a new record in the same sense by his ascent of Aconcagua in the Andes in 1897.

I hesitate to assign any height to Aconcagua; it is said to be a very troublesome mountain to measure, and the elevations which have been assigned to it at different times vary by hundreds of feet. Mr. Vines' party, after much careful work, credited it with 23,100 feet; another very competent and painstaking observer a few years later brought it down to 22,812 feet.

During the past five or six seasons the plot has

[1] *Nature*, vol. xvi. p. 466.

[2] See above, p. 9.

thickened rapidly. In 1908 Dr. William Hunter Workman reached a point on a mountain in Baltistan, some 1100 feet below the summit, for which his aneroid readings gave a height of 23,894 feet, just 12 feet lower than the summit of Trisul. He described this expedition as a "record ascent," in the sense that it was "the highest substantiated ascent yet made in mountaineering."

Then comes Longstaff's attempt on Gurla Mandhata (25,850 feet). At the point where they turned back "the guides both insisted that we were only within 300 metres (1000 feet) of the summit. . . . Personally, I think that we were at least 1500 feet from the top, and therefore less than 24,000 feet above sea-level, but . . . my barometer was broken, and my attempts at boiling the thermometer had been a fiasco, so that all we had to go upon was a comparison of the triangulated peaks around us. It really does not matter what the exact altitude was: even if we had known it, it would not have altered the fact that we were beaten—at least I was."[1] The remark that they were "therefore less than 24,000 feet above sea-level" is a tacit reference to the height of Kabru (24,015 feet), in the ascent of which by Graham, Longstaff has always been a believer.

In 1906 Mrs. Fanny Bullock Workman ascended one of the Nun Kun peaks in Kashmir, 23,264 feet (her husband remained a few hundred feet below the summit taking observations and photographs), and enjoyed for a year the distinction of having attained

[1] *Alpine Journal*, vol. xxiii. p. 223.

the highest summit yet undisputably climbed. She also won the honour, which she is likely to retain considerably longer, of being the only lady among the small list of those who have passed 23,000 feet. Finally, in October 1907, four months after the ascent of Trisul, two Norwegians, Messrs. Rubenson and Monrad-Aas, renewed the attack on Graham's mountain, Kabru, and reached a point within one or two hundred feet of the summit, *i.e.* almost precisely the elevation of W. H. Johnson's peak. These gentlemen secured many excellent photographs, and there is no question of the identity of their mountain, or the precise spot where they turned back; so that if the climbs of Graham and Johnson are to be treated as doubtful, there is no doubt about the validity of their claim to have accomplished "the highest substantiated ascent yet made in mountaineering," if ascent be the proper word to use of an expedition in which the summit of the mountain is not attained.

The subject is complicated, not only by the doubts which overhang the ascents of 1865 and 1883, but also by the uncertainty as to the exact heights reached in each case.

It is well known that the value of calculations based on aneroid readings is only approximate, and must give way to results obtained by triangulation. But the results of triangulation do not always agree, as the case of Aconcagua shows, and even when they practically coincide they cannot be accepted as absolutely unimpeachable: there is good reason to suppose that the effect of refraction is not yet sufficiently understood for the allowances made for it to be perfectly accurate; and the higher or more remote the summit, the larger is the possibility of error. Bearing these facts in mind, and also the small margins of difference between several of the heights above mentioned, it will be apparent that any one who starts to form a decided opinion as to what persons now are, and have in the past been, entitled to the honour of having reached the highest elevations, and made the highest ascents on record, has a very pretty tangle to unravel. And I will "leave it at that." Longstaff lays no claim to any record, and goes out of his way, like a good sportsman, to establish the record of a predecessor.

. . . . . .

Since the preceding pages were written, I have discovered that Trisul itself affords another illustration of the complications referred to in the last paragraph. The height of 23,406 feet is taken from the G.T.S. map, but in the "Sketch of Himalayan Geography and Geology" mentioned on p. 13, it is credited with only 23,360 feet. Through the kindness of one of the authors, Colonel S. C. Burrard, R.E., F.R.S., I have been informed that the former figure is derived from the local topographical observations made by the Kumaon surveyors, the latter from the large triangles of the main Trigonometrical Survey of North India. I gather that the latter figure is probably too low, but that neither can at present be accepted as absolutely final.

# CHAPTER XI

## BACK TO THE DHAULI VALLEY

THE next thing to be done was to get out of the Rishi valley again before our food-supply came to an end; and I at any rate was uncommonly glad that, owing to Bruce's self-sacrificing efforts, we were relieved from the prospect (on which Longstaff had been dwelling with a certain gusto) of having to perform the return journey with double loads, and on half rations. But Bruce, though no longer suffering from fever, was far from well, and badly in need of a rest; it was therefore decided that he should have an off-day, and then go quietly as far as Duti on the 15th. I stayed in camp to keep him company, and try to cheer him up after the dreary boredom and thankless toil of the past fortnight, while Longstaff, indefatigable as usual, started with two Gurkhas to see what the other side of the Rishi chasm was like. He good-naturedly urged that it was my turn, but I knew he wanted to go much more than I did—though for once I did wish to go rather than to sit still—and that the exploring would be more effectively carried out by him.

They went off with a Mummery tent, and very little

else besides some provisions, got down to the Rishi, and ascended its southern bank, not without difficulty, to the entrance of the chasm, opposite the mouth of the Arhamani stream. No farther progress on this side of the Rishi being possible, they crossed it by a bridge of avalanche snow and, making their way up the left bank of the Arhamani stream, selected a camping-ground under an overhanging rock among some birch trees, nearly opposite the place where the Bagini party had camped on May 24. From there they climbed straight up that afternoon, and again next morning, to a height of about 18,500 feet. Nanda Devi was in full view from this side, but "in the intervening 1700 feet of cliffs between this and the Rishi Ganga [they] saw no practicable route up the valley."

There was a tremendous downpour that night and I felt some concern for the plight of the exploring party, but it was quite wasted. When, after recrossing the Rishi, they rejoined us at Duti on the afternoon of the 15th, it appeared that they had greatly enjoyed themselves, and had not even taken the trouble to put up the tent. "Some harmless rain" was the way Longstaff put it in his diary.

Though he has since expressed himself convinced that it is possible to force a way up the Rishi gorge to the western base of Nanda Devi, I think he was not so confident at the time. I adhere to the opinion which I have already expressed, that if the passage is ever made, it will be a *tour de force*, and that it is not a practicable route for a party with any ulterior object in view.

The journey back to the Dhauli valley was quite uneventful, but enjoyable enough, as we were all pleasantly stimulated by the prospect of revelling in a brief orgy of repose amid such luxuries as tea with milk in it, perhaps bread, and possibly jam omelettes, to be followed by the excitement of making a new departure and breaking new ground. The interest in food generated by a sojourn in the mountains is really terrible. Of our appetites at meal-times one can only say that they were Himalayan; and I was so frequently and severely assailed by the pangs of hunger during the intermediate periods, that after a few experiences I made it a rule always, by day and by night, to have some slabs of plasmon chocolate within easy reach. A food question was the only one which now agitated the smooth tenor of our way. When we arrived at Dibrugheta our supplies were very nearly at an end; some one had been sent on to Darashi to bring on the coolies from there, if they *were* there, which was of course by no means a certainty; but the afternoon wore on, and no signs of them were visible. Longstaff went off to try for a musk deer; encountering a tahr, very much to his surprise, he fired at that, *faute de mieux*, and was lured on by the ardour of pursuit to the fearfully steep and difficult ground overhanging the Rishi. The tahr, which was badly hit, fell over a precipice into the river, and Longstaff probably came nearer to a similar fate than on any other occasion in his life. He returned after dark with a lurid narrative of his experiences, but no more solid results.

We rose early next morning, in expectation of a

In the RISHI VALLEY

long day's march right through to Surai Thota. Besides a little cornflour and arrowroot, brought in case of illness, there remained a tongue, which was reserved for tiffin, one tin of biscuits, and three tins of sardines. These latter, grilled with wild garlick, which grew in abundance, provided a savoury if unsubstantial breakfast; we had just finished it and were thinking of starting when the coolies appeared on the skyline between us and Darashi. Shabash!

In these circumstances it would have been flying in the face of Providence to go farther than Darashi, and there we stopped accordingly, spending the afternoon on the spurs which jut out from the plateau and overhang the immense depths of the Rishi gorge.

From Darashi to the Tolma pass took barely two hours' actual walking; the snow on this side had almost disappeared, and it was difficult to believe that this was the passage which had cost so much time and anxiety when we were coming in. By three o'clock we were back again in the big camp. There was a small native caravan on the ground, and with it a young Lama, accompanied by a queer little dog, who paid us a visit at tea-time. Tall, supple, and well-built, in flowing purple raiment, he was a remarkable and striking figure. The distinctive Mongolian traits showed very slightly in his smooth-shaven face, and it was almost handsome and wholly attractive and engaging. He took off his pack, which he carried on his back in a sort of wooden frame, laid it on the ground with his umbrella and a long stick, ending in a kind of plume, then squatted beside us and begged with superb dignity. Bruce gave him a rupee, and after he and Longstaff had made some apparently not very successful essays at conversation, the man rose to go; but Lachman and some of the other men who had gathered round, had evidently looked for something more than this, and after a time he gracefully allowed himself to be persuaded to sit down again and go through the expected performance.

Undoing his pack with deliberate deft rapidity, he produced from it, first, an embroidered yellow garment, cut something like a continuous cape, with a hole in it through which he slipped his head, so that the thing lay on his breast and shoulders; then a pagoda-shaped article, whose use was not apparent till he placed it on his head, where it instantly looked appropriate and effective; lastly, something resembling a small triptych, except that it had five folds instead of three, carved and gilded all over, with a little picture of Buddha in each fold—this he spread out and stuck neatly into the front of the pagoda above his forehead, giving somewhat the effect of a crown.

The show was now complete, and he sat perfectly still for a few minutes, with a beaming smile on his face, turning his praying machine the while; then with the same deliberate swiftness took all the things off, packed them neatly away, and again passed round the hat.

This time he made his application to Inderbinen, whose stare of embarrassed helplessness was not the least amusing thing in the entertainment; however, he was provided with material for a donation, and the Lama, still preserving a dignified serenity, saluted slightly and walked off up the Niti road. We made out that he was bound for a monastery near Gyantse, but he reappeared next day with a party of Tibetans travelling south ; as to his arrival at the monastery, he was probably not particular to a month or so.

Surai Thota, wind swept and dusty, and fouled by many native caravans, was no fit place on which to enjoy an orgy of repose. For that purpose we moved on to Juma Gwar, and spent two days there without stirring. All were glad of the rest, and looked upon it as well earned, though the amount of walking done by the whole party, except Longstaff, during the past six days was, judged by Swiss standards, by no means severe, and we ought to have been—and in the Alps no doubt would have been—bursting with an accumulation of fresh energy. Every one, however, was by now in the best of health, with the exception of Kharbir, who was paying the penalty for his pluck and resolution in going up Trisul, and suffering severely from the effects of frost-bite.

Many letters were written, and much washing was got through (we had fallen sadly into arrear in the matter of washing, not only of our clothes but of ourselves) ; each of us sooner or later, Alexis included, waxed autobiographical, and favoured the others with large fragments of his past history. Future plans were discussed with ample and pleasant vagueness. The months stretched ahead in a long vista—July, August, September. It was just eight weeks since the start from Almora, and we had nearly twice that time before us. It seemed almost more than we knew what to do with.

We should have been greatly surprised to be told that most of our work in Garhwal was already accomplished, and that all the party but one would be back in Almora in less than seven weeks more.

The start for new ground commenced inauspiciously, for rain was falling when the march began, for the first time since we started; but it did not last. The mouth of the Bagini valley was soon passed, and then for two hours the walk was decidedly dull, till a gorge was reached longer and wilder, though less striking, than that of Juma Gwar. Here we met a Tibetan and his wife with a pack-mule, and Longstaff saluted them in customary Tibetan fashion—that is to say, he put out his tongue at them. They stared for a second or two, a little taken aback, and then they laughed. How they laughed!—their bright little eyes twinkling, and their bodies shaking and quivering all over, as though nothing so richly and exquisitely funny had ever happened before. It seems inconceivable that intercourse with such mirth-loving people could be otherwise than friendly if their attitude was not determined by orders from above. There was nothing else of any interest till near the end of the walk, when we passed the glen which leads to the Kosa glacier. The quaint little village of Kosa stands picturesquely at its mouth, but the entrance behind the village is so narrow that no idea can be obtained from the road of what lies beyond. It had never been contemplated that we should visit this valley; indeed, it was not till we traversed the Kuari pass and, like Graham, were surprised by the crowd of bold inaccessible-looking peaks immediately across the Dhauli valley, that we took any interest at all in the southern half of the Kamet range; even now I know nothing of the interior of the Kosa basin beyond what can be learnt from an inspection of the map. It is very large, apparently containing an icefield of an area at least equal in extent to the Bagini glacier; it gives access to several great peaks, one of which attains the respectable altitude of 22,141 feet, and it seems the obvious place from which to commence the exploration of this half of the range; but, though it may have been visited by sportsmen, I am inclined to think that no European, certainly no one bent on exploration, has penetrated its recesses since the surveyors. I cannot imagine a more fascinating programme for a party arriving at Tapoban, as we did, early in May, than to start with the Juma glen, and then when its possibilities were exhausted, to devote themselves to a thorough investigation of the peaks and glaciers of the Kosa valley. Later on we came to regard it with much more attention and curiosity, but at this time we bestowed on it only a passing glance, and, after a slight ascent, found that the march was nearly over, and that we were looking over the beautiful basin of Malari. At the first view the Dhauli valley appeared to end in a *cul de sac*: lofty hills, flecked with snow near the skyline, and descending in immense grassy slopes to brown terraces of cultivated land, surrounded an extensive plateau elevated considerably above the river bed; their vast sweep was scarcely broken by two narrow clefts, out of one of which the Girthi river emerges from its struggle through a gorge which rivals that of the Rishi; by the other the Dhauli forces its way down close under the wonderfully serrated rock-wall which encloses the Kosa basin on its northern side.

There was an unusual air of geniality and friendliness, and a gratifying sense of space and elbow-room about the whole landscape, and one was not surprised to find in this oasis by far the most considerable and prosperous-looking village that we had yet seen in Garhwal. The houses were not only substantially built, but elaborately and tastefully decorated with wood-carving to an extent which, especially when it is remembered that they are only occupied for half the year, implies the existence of strong artistic impulses in their owners. Malari is the most important seat in the Niti valley of that curious little people, the Bhotias, who deserve a brief introduction here. Numerically insignificant, they are of great interest to the ethnologist, and much has been written about them. Their principal habitations are the upper portions of the Mana, Niti, and Milam valleys (I never could discover exactly where they betake themselves in the winter); a small section lives farther east, close to Nepal. They are of Tibetan origin, and their dialects are Tibeto-Burman; in religion they are by way of being Hindus, and it is said that they are being steadily Hinduised, but they still retain many local customs and superstitions peculiar to themselves, and many of them eat and drink freely with the Tibetans; it is owing in part to this practice, partly to racial and linguistic affinities, that they have succeeded in establishing an absolute

MALARI.

monopoly of trade with Tibet, along the Garhwal-Kumaon frontier line. From Malari onwards, till we left the Mana valley, all our porters were Bhotias.

Between Malari and Niti there is a regular knot of ranges and ridges, through and across which the Girthi and Dhauli rivers have cut their way in a fashion of which it is almost hopeless to give any idea by a verbal description.

The Niti pass road follows the tortuous course of the Dhauli through a gorge which has been already mentioned, and of which Longstaff, who had come down it in 1905, spoke very highly; but we chose a more elevated route, just to the north of it, up the western slope of the Malari basin and over the Kurkuti Dhar (15,064 feet), hoping to get some photographs of Dunagiri and the mountains on the north-east of the Bagini glacier, and a near prospect of the Kosa peaks.

The way this walk was taken by the different members of the party was characteristic. Bruce went ahead with two Gurkhas at a tremendous rate, without resting or pausing till he reached the skyline; I followed *longo intervallo* with two more Gurkhas and Inderbinen, who was carrying the eatables, till I was quite overpowered by hunger. I sent on the Gurkhas with Bruce's share, but before they overtook him he had started on the way down, quite regardless of such matters as tiffin; last of all came Longstaff, at a speed governed by forethought and deliberate intention. It sounds very easy to go more slowly than one's natural pace, but to do so for hours together is, in fact, very irksome, and requires a great deal of self-control. I gave the practice just sufficient trial to be convinced that it results, at high levels, in a very appreciable saving of strength, and that the habit of it is worth cultivating.

As we ascended, the unspeakably desolate and savage valley of the Girthi was visible for some miles; but very little could be seen of the higher regions, and I almost regretted not having gone by the road. The amount and variety of picturesque valley scenery packed into this complicated little bit of country is really astonishing; however, opportunities of becoming better acquainted with it in detail came later, and it was well worth while crossing the ridge in order to obtain a grasp of its general configuration.

From the summit-ridge we looked down about 5000 feet on to the Niti road and the river. This short bit of the Dhauli is completely shut off from the rest of its course, both above and below, and is continuous with a broad trough-like valley, which runs up into the heart of the Kamet range and leads to the depression which we traversed later. This valley was visible for several miles, and provided the one feature in the view which was not spoiled by clouds.

The main Dhauli valley lies more to the east, separated from the trough by a ridge which joins on to the hills of the Malari basin a few hundred yards from where we were standing. The passage which the river has sliced through it from the one valley to the other is, perhaps, the most striking of its many gorges.

We glissaded in a few minutes to the gap at the

point of junction, and found so much snow on the northern slopes that the descent to the camping-ground of Timor Shim, opposite the mouth of the gorge, took scarcely an hour. Longstaff pointed out the track from the Chor Hoti pass by which he had returned

to Indian territory two years before, and a group of insignificant birch trees, over which he and the Brocherels had been quite excited after some weeks in the arid Tibetan plains. I should not have noticed their existence if he had not drawn my attention to them; the place struck me as bare and dreary, entirely devoid of the charm and verdure of Malari, and visibly marking another stage nearer to the absolute dryness of the regions beyond the watershed. There is, however, a considerable extent of level cultivable ground, and Niti, about one and a half miles above Timor Shim, the highest of the Bhotia villages, and the one from which the pass takes its name, looks as substantially built and comfortable as Malari, and not much inferior in size; the wood-carving, which I had an opportunity of examining closely, seemed to be even more curious and picturesque.

Half-bred yaks or jibbus are used for transport from Niti onwards, and Bruce made arrangements for hiring them; but some of them had to be fetched from a distance, and it was necessary to spend a second day at Timor Shim before a sufficient number could be collected. There was some talk of going up Hoti peak, a summit of 18,874 feet near the Chor Hoti pass; but the ascent would have had no mountaineering interest, and the idea was abandoned.

On June 26 we got under weigh with eighteen yaks and fourteen coolies, leaving the main camp behind in charge of Kharbir, who was still crippled and in pain.

The river above Niti runs in a deep precipitous channel, along the cliffs of which, we were informed, is a track practicable for pedestrians, with a *mauvais pas*; but the road for yaks, which we followed, is carried high above the river on the left bank (though not quite high enough for any distant prospect), till one arrives suddenly at a point overlooking the next open level stretch of valley—the pasture-ground of Goting.

NITI VILLAGE.

Above Goting the valley forks: the Niti road turns off to the right (north-east); on the left is the opening which leads to the Raikana glacier and Kamet, so the end of our journey in this direction was almost in sight. On the slope descending to the valley floor were a few birch trees—the very last; Longstaff observed that the character of the landscape had grown by yet another degree more purely Tibetan, and the change was apparent even to an unpractised eye. Straight ahead of us, between the main Niti valley and the Raikana glacier, rose a great mountain mass, culminating in a summit called Chango, 20,216 feet. On this peak too we had cherished designs, but we were not taking much interest in climbing anything only 20,000 feet high, unless it proved to be intrinsically attractive, and Chango struck us all as being so deeply uninteresting that it was at once dismissed from the list of possibilities.

As we were descending to the camping-ground one of the yaks indulged in a little mild buck-jumping. They seldom break out in this way, but when they do so something usually comes off, and in a few seconds a *kilta* [1] was bounding down the hillside, and pots of jam, tins of chocolate and similar articles flew about in all directions. Most of them were recovered intact; but it was an agitating moment, and one could not stifle the private reflection, "There, but for a kindly Providence, goes my lyte wate."

[1] A pannier or basket.

## CHAPTER XII

### THE RAIKANA GLACIER AND KAMET

EVERY one was astir very early next morning, and I was up and out with what I considered commendable speed, but it did not satisfy the two Gurkhas, who were waiting hungrily outside my tent, ready to take it down and pack it the instant I was dressed. It is extraordinary how powerful and stimulating is the moral effect produced by a pair of silent figures gazing impassively but expectantly at nothing as one lies in bed. Not the laziest of mortals could stand it for long.

The reason for urgency turned out to be that it was necessary to leave the Niti pass road and get over at once to the right bank of the Dhauli; the yaks must wade through the river unencumbered, while the loads had to be carried across by the men and packed on the other side. The way over for the latter was by a natural boulder bridge a little below the camp, at the entrance of the narrow channel of which mention has been already made; it was a ticklish place for loaded people, and fully two hours and a half elapsed before everything was safely over and the yaks loaded up.

In about an hour more we reached the junction of

Looking Southward from the
Raikhana Glacier.

the Dhauli and Raikana streams, and crossed the latter by a bridge of avalanche snow. Not long afterwards some barhal were sighted, and the whole caravan pulled up for some time to watch a stalk, so that I have no record of the day's "times"; but the rest of the march cannot have been much more than one and a half hours' actual walking. We halted at a pleasant piece of flat ground, with good water and fuel

in unexpected plenty. Screes on a large scale—a novel feature—extended far up the valley on our right: in front the glacier was hidden by a gigantic terminal moraine, above which showed snowy peaks; beyond the skyline was Tibet. The place is called Kali Kharak (*c.* 18,600 feet); the true Raikana Kharak, which we thought we had reached, lies an hour or two farther on, and five or six hundred feet higher. We passed it next day, climbed to the top of the big mass of moraine, and soon reached snow. The surface was so uneven that in places the yaks required a good deal of shoving from behind to get them up, and so thickly strewn with débris and boulders that it was impossible to tell where the glacier began. We finally pitched the camp on the left bank, at a height of 15,350 feet, in what looked like a sheltered spot, but was not; it turned out to be a regular cauldron of the winds, and on more than one occasion, after I had been sitting in the afternoon on places apparently far more exposed, and finding everything calm and still, I returned to find a vigorous breeze blowing round the tents.

I speak feelingly, for I spent five days at this place without achieving more than a walk of an hour or two up the glacier, and during the first two days at least feeling quite unfit for anything further. "Mountain lassitude" is a phrase which belongs peculiarly to our party: it was invented by Bruce; Longstaff, in his monograph on *Mountain Sickness*, has approved of and adopted it; it was left for me to illustrate its ravages. The mental condition produced by it is one of extreme readiness to discuss the most strenuous programmes for next week, and a profound reluctance to do anything to-day or to-morrow. There is, I think, no doubt that this most demoralising effect of high altitudes varies without any apparent reason in different localities. The natives certainly hold this opinion. They still adhere to the view that mountain sickness in all its phases is caused by the poisonous exhalations of a mysterious plant, which is supposed to grow in places where the symptoms of the affection manifest themselves, and they look upon some of the high passes as more exposed to this evil influence than others. Prob-

The RAIKHANA GLACIER looking west.

THE RAIKHANA GLACIER, LOOKING WEST

ably they don't trouble to go more deeply than this into the matter, but once the plant hypothesis is accepted it is easy to go a step further, and assume that it grows more abundantly in some places than in others. Those who do not find this explanation satisfactory must be content to accept the bare fact. Certain it is that, for some reason or other, the place disagreed with me, and Inderbinen was not in much better case. I therefore saw nothing at close quarters of the inner recesses of the chain where rise the giants Kamet, Mana peak, No. 1 (28,862 feet), and the mountain (24,170) discovered by Sir R. Strachey. The Raikana glacier itself is, like the Bagini and Trisul glaciers, a huge ice-stream with a very gradual slope, and for some miles completely hidden by piled-up moraine débris, the ice only showing here and there. We only ascertained by degrees that it certainly extends much farther down than it is represented to do in the G.T.S. map, and well below the camping-ground. It gradually merges in an extensive field of névé, closed by a range of snowy mountains of no great elevation, in which is a well-marked col, clearly to be attained without difficulty from this side by long slopes of snow, and probably giving easy access to Tibet. There was some talk of an expedition to this col, for my special benefit, as I had a natural desire to get, for once, as far as the Tibetan frontier, and set a foot inside the forbidden land. The glacier is bounded on the east by the face of the rocky mass which forms the pedestal of the despised Chango—low and shelving where it abuts on the upper reaches of the ice-stream, but from the camping-ground downwards, where the valley falls away, rising in steep cliffs, which tower to a quite imposing altitude over the screes which I have already mentioned; the ends of some small glaciers are just visible above them, "rimming the rock row," and

exquisitely transparent and beautiful when they are illumined by the morning sun.

On the west, two large lateral glaciers join the principal one; the more southerly of the two is very similar to it in character, being long, level, and extremely dirty, so much so indeed that the moraine-covered surface seems to have led the surveyors to believe that it did not join the main ice-stream. This glacier, which Longstaff has named the Kamet glacier, and the mouth of which was nearly opposite the camp, leads past the northern base of Mana peak to the foot of Kamet; the other, the more northerly, runs up to Sir R. Strachey's peak. The ridges which enclose them are squat and dumpy in appearance. A far smaller glacier comes in lower down, surrounded by minor heights, where alone are to be found some effect of height and some boldness of outline.

No greater contrast could be imagined to the mighty walls and the stupendous heights and depths of the Nanda Devi range, yet, though the elements of grandeur and sublimity are absent, the scene has an impressiveness and individuality of its own, and is free from any suggestion of the monotony and dreariness which one associates with arctic landscape, and which one finds (I judge only from photographs) on the other side, in the neighbourhood of the Mana pass. In spite of climatic drawbacks the Raikana glacier is worth seeing, and worth going to see, though I must own that, if I ever found myself in the Dhauli valley again, it is the last place there which I should wish to revisit.

The day after our arrival, Longstaff went up the glacier with the Brocherels to make a reconnaissance. He returned at 6.30, after a long and tiring day, during which he had suffered considerably from headache and difficulty in breathing, with an extremely discouraging report as to the possibility of getting up any of the peaks from this side. They had been as far as the mouth of the northern glacier, and located peak 24,170 feet, at the head of it; Longstaff is inclined to think that this peak, and not Kamet, is the Ibi Gamin of the

Schlagintweits. Returning, they had gone some distance up the Kamet glacier, and had seen enough to show that they were on the only route by which Kamet could be approached; the upper extremity of the glacier was not visible, as, according to the map, it ought to have been, and it was desirable, as a matter of topographical interest, that an expedition should be made

to examine further into this point, but that anything beyond this could be achieved was more than doubtful.

This narrative resulted in a council of war; Bruce had been devoting the day to making arrangements for a move on the morrow on a large scale, with three Whymper tents and a week's provisions, but in the face of Longstaff's report this seemed scarcely worth while, and he now proposed to send word at once to Lachman at Goting to return with the yaks and their attendants to Raikana Kharak, with a view to leaving on the 3rd or 4th of July; should Kamet turn out to be unexpectedly get-at-able, it would always be open to us to reconsider the position. This plan was attractively convenient from the standpoint of *bandobast*; I hailed it with unabashed satisfaction, though it involved abandoning the ascent of the Tibetan pass; and I believe that Bruce and Longstaff were also touched by the malign influence of the place, and not sorry to cut short their stay.

They started next morning (June 30) for the Kamet glacier with the Brocherels, six Gurkhas, and ten coolies to carry up tents, etc.; at a height of 16,800 feet a grassy slope, *mirabile dictu*, was found to camp on, and the coolies returned. Bruce was unwell that night and unable to go farther, but the others, including Damar Sing with his plane-table, reached the desired point, something over 20,000 feet. Their exertions were very ill rewarded, for clouds and an icy wind rendered plane-tabling impossible, and hid the great south-east face of Kamet, but the upper portion of the Kamet glacier, winding from its foot, was duly inspected; it is a mere death-trap, lying in so narrow a gorge that it would be impossible to avoid the avalanches which constantly fall into it.

The hopelessness of attacking Kamet or Mana peak from the Raikana glacier was established beyond question, and on July 3 we returned to Goting, with the intention of crossing the range to the valley of the Vishnu river, and the hope that these peaks might prove to be more approachable from the western side:

in other words, from the Mana pass route. From Goting, by way of variety, we took the short-cut to Niti which I have already mentioned, along the cliffs overhanging the Dhauli river. It will be remembered that there was said to be a *mauvais pas* on this route. My experience of the Garhwalis had led me to believe that when they say a place is bad it *is* bad, and it was

fully confirmed on this occasion. The whole walk is rather sensational, and the *mauvais pas* quite deserves its reputation; I was uncommonly glad that I had not to traverse it alone.

During our absence the main camp had been shifted down from Timor Shim through the Niti gorge, and was now established near the village of Gamsali, at the upper end of the isolated portion of the Dhauli valley which lies between the Niti gorge and the one leading to the Malari basin. Kharbir, still crippled though no longer suffering, was waiting to welcome us, and we brought some good news for him; the post which had reached us at Goting on the way up contained, amongst other items, a letter addressed to

"Subadar Kharbir," and informing him that he had received his promotion to that rank. It was a great pleasure to us to congratulate so stout a mountaineer and so good a comrade on his attainment of this coveted distinction, the highest attainable by a native soldier; and we made the occasion a pretext for a mild orgy that evening.

# CHAPTER XIII

## COLONEL SMYTH'S PASS[1]

THE two following days were spent in idleness at Gamsali. Every one wanted a short spell at a lower level to recuperate; indeed, somebody threw out the appalling suggestion that I required more, and ought to go round with the main camp *via* Joshimath if I wished to be in good trim for the hoped-for ascent of Kamet from the west; but I recoiled, fortunately, from this drastic measure.

The scenery of this cut-off section of the Dhauli is very grand, in a sombre gloomy style, especially towards the lower end, where the river curves round towards Malari, and the valley is closed by a dark rock-ridge of unusually bold and striking outline, draped with a mantle of pine forests which in the sunlight shone like green velvet. Above its towers and pinnacles there appeared occasionally a snowy curtain, looking incredibly high, which must be part of Dunagiri. The valley is continued above Gamsali in the form of a straight flat-bottomed trough, fully half a mile in

[1] I have chosen this chapter heading in preference to "The Bhyundar Pass," in the hope that the name "Smyth's pass," like "Traill's pass," may become permanent, and serve to commemorate Colonel Smyth's work as the pioneer of mountaineering in Garhwal. His graphic and interesting account of his passage is given in General Macintyre's *Hindu-Koh*, p. 384.

breadth, which we had viewed from the Kurkuti Dhar pass, and which Longstaff has aptly compared to the Lauterbrunnen valley. It leads to a great glacier running up into the heart of the chain, unnamed, but called by the Gamsali people Banke Gal. Over one of the feeders of this glacier lies Colonel Smyth's Bhyundar pass, by which we hoped to reach

the Mana valley. It was proposed to send the main camp and heavy baggage round to Mana in charge of Kharbir, who was still unfit for snow and ice work; this meant returning to Tapoban, and going round by Joshimath up the Vishnu valley, eight or nine days' marching; it also involved the employment of a large number of coolies, besides those required for the pass, so, before finally committing ourselves, a little preliminary investigation seemed desirable.

We started accordingly on July 7 with some Gamsali coolies, leaving the main camp where it was. Piles of broken crags rose on our right, their summit ridges shattered and riven, and showing every sign of rock-falls on a vast scale at no very remote period. The track threaded its way through a wilderness of monstrous boulders, which covered great spaces of the valley floor. On the opposite side towered an imposing wall of black cliffs, the outer bulwark of the Kosa basin; it was seamed by terrific couloirs, in which the snow had hardened into small glaciers of extraordinary steepness. The boulders came to an end, and a delightful green oasis sloped gently up, spreading right across the valley, and rising considerably higher than the stony plain beyond it. It is an unmistakable terminal moraine, which (I am quoting here from our geological member) "can only have been formed at a time when the snout of its parent glacier was almost stationary, or only retreating very very slowly. After this the glacier must have retreated with great rapidity back to its present point of termination (18,000 feet), about which it has made another stand, as evidenced by the formation and character of its moraines. The intermediate distance is a flat waste of stones, through which the stream wanders in many channels, but the lateral moraines are still well marked where side-streams and avalanches have not destroyed them. The secondary glaciers coming down from the G.T.S. peak, 19,815 feet, formerly joined the main glacier, and even now come down much lower than is indicated on the map."[1]

[1] *Geographical Journal*, vol. xxxi. p. 381.

RATABAN.

The glaciers here referred to are on the right as one goes up the valley, and are really not indicated on the map at all. The summit of the ridge on which they lie could be reached without difficulty, and it is quite possible that a pass might be effected across it which would lead to Goting.

The valley turns due west some distance before the Banke glacier is reached. A fine snowy peak was visible at its head for a few minutes, 21,198 of the G.T.S. map, and then came into view a very steep rocky mass with a dome-shaped snow-cap, which, however, turned out later to be only a buttress or offshoot of point 21,198 feet.

About an hour after turning the corner we arrived at Thur Udiar, and camped there, at a height of about 13,000 feet; this place is represented as being close to the snout of the glacier, but it is now at least 500 yards below it. Next day we took to the left-hand lateral moraine, and in an hour and a quarter got a good view of Rataban and a nearly level glacier at its base, which flows into the main Banke glacier, and leads up to Colonel Smyth's pass. Rataban, an exceedingly beautiful peak of 20,094 feet, is the culminating point of the northern bulwark of the Kosa basin. We had thought that it might turn out to be possible to combine an ascent of it with the crossing of the pass, but all hopes of this were dissipated by the first sight of the mountain.

A short distance beyond the junction of the two glaciers the main one turns northward; we rounded a sharp rocky corner, which cut off from sight the glacier and valley behind us, and, a few minutes later, came to a halt, after a very leisurely walk of two and a half hours, on a flat shelf called Eri Udiar, *i.e.* "Cold Cave," exactly opposite point 21,198 and its snow-capped buttress.

The name suggests discomfort, but in fact it was a charming spot, sheltered yet sunny, and with good

water hard by. Its height was 14,690 feet, less than 700 feet lower than the camp on the Raikana glacier; but the whole feel of the place was different, and the breathing trouble, always present there, vanished entirely.

After a depressing day of clouds and rain, which kept everybody but Longstaff at home, he and Bruce went back to Gamsali to make final arrangements. The rest of us went up the glacier as far as the foot

THE AIGUILLE CIRQUE.

of a tremendous icefall, where at last there was a fairly good opportunity for the Brocherels to give the Gurkhas some schooling in ice-work. They spent a couple of hours happily, and I hope usefully, cutting steps in the blue ice of some fine seracs, while I took photographs, as well as the clouds and a dull day permitted. I was particularly interested in a beautiful semicircular bay, which I nicknamed the "Aiguille Cirque," and which positively bristled with dark spires and pinnacles; a glacier descended at an extremely steep angle down the middle of them, and, spreading over the floor of the bay, joined the main ice-stream. We could here see some way farther up the glacier, which curved to the west, but it disappeared again round a corner to the right; and another walk up it to see the girdle of rocky walls which the map showed enclosing its head, appeared to be the most profitable way of spending the following day. I felt so much better here, that if there had been two days to play with I should have tried to organise a more serious expedition; but the others were likely to return at once, and I was rather shy of undertaking a really hard day with the Bhyundar pass—an unknown quantity—immediately to follow.

It was so fine early next morning that I got out of bed without waiting for any outside stimulus, and went up to the ledge above the camp with a camera, and with Longstaff's paradox on the chance of surprising some ram-chicor. Of course the ram-chicor were not there, but my burst of energy was amply rewarded, for I not only got a most glorious view, but had the satisfaction of seeing that if I had dallied, even for a few minutes, I should have been robbed of it by rising mists. The illustrations will show that I was only just in time. Before I had finished photographing, Inderbinen appeared, following me like a careful hen after a missing chicken. After breakfast we took things easily—too easily, as it turned out. We crossed the glacier, and had a look at the quaint little lake shown on the map

at the foot of the buttress of point 21,198. Colonel Smyth mentions but did not visit it; it is a genuine lake, completely separated from the glacier. Snow-pigeon swarmed about its banks, and something which looked like a stone man stood at its far end, but I was not near enough to be certain about this. Going up the moraine to the western bend, we struck across the glacier again, towards the corner of which I have already spoken. The weather had been going from bad to worse, and now snow began to fall, so there was nothing to be done but take shelter under a boulder and wait. Time went by and Inderbinen wanted to go back, but there were still occasional gleams of sun, and finally we got to the corner about four o'clock. Some gentle snow-slopes rose in front of us, hiding the view up the glacier, but there was blue sky visible beyond them, and

—most unexpectedly—nothing showing above them. It was now Inderbinen's turn to feel the explorer's ardour, and, to my great amusement, he entirely changed his tune, saying, "We *must* go on as far as the skyline; I daresay we shall be back before it gets dark."

So on we went; it was not much more than a quarter of an hour to a point from which we could see the glacier again. Some little way up it there was a sort of small icefall, descending from nothing in particular; and beyond that—a good way beyond it—a line of low ice-capped mountain, rising on the right to much greater heights, which were lost in clouds, but on the left dropping abruptly. Meanwhile the ridge bounding the glacier on its true right (our left hand), which in the G.T.S. map continues unbroken to Mana peak, came to

an end, so that there was a fairly broad gap, apparently lower than where we were standing, between the end of it and the ice-capped line in front of us. Was there a low col round to the left leading to one of the lateral glaciers of the Mana valley? Or was it possible that the summit of the little icefall before us was itself the main watershed, and that another glacier on the far side of it descended through the gap into a side valley? It certainly looked as if this was the case. Indeed, if I am right in supposing that the glacier *sinks* to the gap beyond the little icefall, then it seems to follow as a matter of physical necessity. Some interesting matters are involved in the correct answer to this question: in the first place, if my assumption is correct, the descent through the gap, if practicable, offers the most direct route to the Mana pass road, which it would apparently strike four or five miles above Mana village, without the necessity of crossing any secondary ridge, as must be done when the Bhyundar pass is taken. There may, of course, be difficulties in the way—impracticable ice-falls and impassable gorges, for instance; but, judging by the general character of the larger low-lying glaciers, the presence of the former at any rate is improbable. Then, secondly, what becomes of the watershed between the little icefall and Mana peak? I am sorely tempted to hazard some speculative conjectures on this subject, but I will content myself with saying that an exploration of the region between the Raikana and Banke glaciers would probably yield some interesting surprises. I would have given a good deal to be able to put the clock back two or three hours; but we had no lantern, and it was no use thinking of going on any farther.

Night was closing in when we got back, and Bruce and Longstaff were looking out for us: everything had been satisfactorily arranged, and a sufficient number of coolies had been collected, but it had not been altogether an easy matter to bring the coolies for the Bhyundar pass up to the scratch, and the order had gone forth for a start next morning, for it was possible that they might not face it if they were not taken over at once. I remarked that I was feeling rather tired, and that I should not mind if we were delayed by a storm. "If there 's a storm to-morrow morning," said Longstaff, with conviction, "the coolies will bolt."

Nothing, however, went wrong, and the three days that followed provided an unbroken spell of pure enjoyment. Friday, July 12, broke cloudlessly. Half a dozen barhal of varying sizes and ages paid us a farewell visit, peering curiously down over the edge of the shelf above the camping-ground as we sat at breakfast. Giving the coolies a good start, we set off at about seven o'clock.

In a little over two hours we were well up the side glacier, right under the superb north face of Rataban, and within sight of the ascent to the pass. The best way lies up some steepish slopes of rock and stones on the right, giving access to the snowy plateau which slopes gently up to the col. Colonel Smyth crossed the pass in 1862, on the last day of October. He had of course no maps at all, and had to rely on the guidance of the padhan of Gamsali, who had only been over once before, many years previously, in the month of July, under very different snow conditions; perhaps, too, the glacier has altered since. At all events, the party failed to hit upon this route, as they found the upper part of the glacier very steep and very much crevassed; they had to cut steps with axes nearly the whole way, and only reached the col a little before sunset.

Three barhal came over the col soon after our arrival on the plateau, and approached within seventy or

The BHYUNDAR PASS.

eighty yards, then after a pause for mutual inspection, beat a leisurely retreat. We reached the summit level of the pass about mid-day, in four hours' easy walking from Eri Udiar. Its height comes out at 16,700 feet only, but there are reasons for supposing that it is really considerably more. The best of the day was over, and little could be seen of the Badrinath peaks beyond the Vishnu valley, but I do not think that under the most favourable conditions there would be a good panoramic view. The most interesting objects before us were the peaks immediately to the south, at the head of the basin of the Kosa glacier. One craggy top, which looked quite close to us, towered above the ridge that descends from Rataban, and a lovely white mountain stood out finely to the right, some distance away.

I take the craggy top to be point 21,747 feet of the G.T.S. map, but I am in a state of great perplexity with regard to the white mountain, and indeed, with regard to the topography generally on the south-western side of the pass, as will presently appear. The map is very sketchy here, giving no idea of the dimensions of the Thiap-ka-bank or Bhyundar glacier, which commences just to the south of the pass and almost on a level with it, tumbles over a belt of cliffs into a large ice-basin, and then pursues its way for some miles down the Bhyundar glen. Only the last stage of it is represented on the map, which, moreover, omits altogether two lateral glaciers on the southern side of the Bhyundar glen, which will be mentioned in due course later on. On the far side of the glacier a huge rocky promontory thrusts itself out, which I believe to be a continuation of the Rataban ridge; but Longstaff has identified it—wrongly, as I think—with the Lakpal of the G.T.S. map, with the result that he has greatly exaggerated its extension westward.

The descent of the pass is far steeper and longer than the ascent; one is soon brought to a stop by the rocky belt, and it is not surprising that Colonel Smyth's party, overtaken by darkness, again got into difficulties, and had to spend the night within 200 or 800 feet of the top of the pass without firewood, water, or food, or cover of any kind. "The cold," he says, "affected them in various ways: some had a violent headache, others were sick all night." This sounds like the effect of altitude rather than of cold. They were all unable to start till 10 A.M., "when the sun made its appearance from behind 'Goree Purbut.' The cold was so intense that we could not touch the rocks with our hands." Even then their troubles were not over; in several places they had to let one another down by ropes, and did not reach the foot of the precipice until 2 or 8 P.M.

We found a fairly easy way down a rock gully some distance to the right, which our predecessor seems to have missed; but there were some steep snow-slopes to traverse first, and big steps had to be cut for the coolies. One man slipped and slid down at a great pace, but he was neatly fielded by Henri Brocherel before he had gone very far.

It must have taken a little over an hour to get to the bottom of the steep descent, and about half an hour more to cross the broad plateau of the ice-basin.

Here we stopped for some time to take in at leisure one of the wildest and most imposing pieces of scenery that I have ever come across. We had got beyond the end of the "Lakpal" promontory, and quite suddenly there came into view another large glacier flowing along the base of peak 21,747, and joining the main ice-stream at right angles; we could see right up it to a

well-defined col at its head, which Longstaff represents as crossing the chain to the Juma glacier, but which I should have expected to lead into the Kosa basin; from its right bank the western face of point 21,747 shot up in one sheer precipice to the summit, 9000 feet above. In the whole of our travels we met no spectacle more impressive than this tremendous wall.

Leaving the glacier at this point we went for two

or three miles along the side of the Bhyundar valley, and at 3.30 camped at the foot of deliciously green grass slopes on a little sandy flat snugly tucked in between them and the right-hand lateral moraine, which completely hid the glacier from view. This spot is known as Shem Kharak; though it is nearly 2000 feet lower than at Eri Udiar, I had a slight recurrence of the breathing trouble that night, probably a result of the strain of two fairly long days in succession.

We passed the snout of the Bhyundar glacier next morning in about three-quarters of an hour, at a height of 12,000 feet. There were no traces of the Lakpal-ka-kund lake of the G.T.S. map. It was again a brilliant day, and the luxuriant meadows were ablaze with flowers. Longstaff enumerates ferns, yellow lilies, and anemones, green fritillaries, purple monkshood, and in the drier spots a beautiful blue dwarf iris and white and red wild strawberries, with forget-me-nots and large yellow king-cups by the streams; I have a pleasing recollection of wild onions as well.

Henri said, quite truly, that it was like Switzerland; Bruce pronounced it to be a piece of Kashmir, and to Longstaff it recalled scenes in Suanetia; while Inderbinen's economic mind wandered off into calculations about the number of cows that the place would support, and regrets over the deplorable waste of pasturage. Certainly the change from the prevailing arid bareness of the upper valley of the Dhauli was extraordinarily striking, and the eye revelled in the refreshing greenery.

The valley appeared to be hemmed in on all sides: high up on the right (north) was a row of craggy summits, embracing three lofty glaciers of quite respectable dimensions. The slopes on the south were not nearly so steep, and in one of their hollows lay a good-sized glacier—the second of those referred to above—extending nearly to the valley floor, below the point where the Bhyundar glacier comes to an end.

Straight ahead of us was next day's col; at its foot the valley makes an extremely sharp turn—nearly a right angle—to the left (south), and the stream vanishes down a lovely wooded gorge, which reminded one of bits of the Rishi valley, to join the Vishnu river many miles below, near Pandukeswar. We were told that there was no way up this gorge; if this is so, and our two passes are the only entrances to this delectable place, it is no wonder that it is unfrequented. Here at the corner, after a most enjoyable walk of two hours, we halted for the day, at an altitude of 11,650 feet. Our coolies named the place Bhamini Daur.

I must here sum up my views with reference to certain topographical points, as I am not at all happy about this portion of our map. It will be noticed that Longstaff has given to the two peaks 21,747 feet and 22,141 feet the names of Gauri Parbat and Hathi Parbat respectively, but he has left unaltered the positions in which they are placed on the G.T.S. map. He did no plane-tabling on this occasion, and as these peaks have been triangulated, he has accepted them as fixed points, and has made, on that basis, the alterations necessary to introduce the two new lateral glaciers. Nevertheless, I am quite unable to reconcile the relative positions of these peaks and of Rataban with my recollections and notes, or with our photographs, and at the risk of being convicted at some future date of being hopelessly deficient in the topographical sense, I will put my own impressions on record for what they are worth.

I believe that peaks 21,747 and 22,141 and the "Lakpal" promontory should be much nearer to Rataban, and that it results from the misplacing of

these two peaks and the undue extension of "Lakpal" that the southern boundary ridge of the Bhyundar valley is thrust much too far back, and that the two new glaciers are shown as commencing farther southward, and both they and the Bhyundar glacier itself as finishing much farther westward, than is really the case. Bhamini Daur is certainly well below (west of) the second of them.

As to the white mountain, I am inclined to think that it is Colonel Smyth's "Goree Purbut," which he speaks of as that "peculiar-looking flat-topped mountain, so distinctly visible from Almora, Pauri, and the plains"; but I feel very doubtful as to its being visible from Almora, and think that there may be some confusion with Nanda Ghunti, to which it bears a remarkable resemblance. Longstaff, if I understand him rightly, identifies it with his Hathi Parbat (22,141). I will hazard the conjecture that it is distinct from both Gauri Parbat and Hathi Parbat, and stands well to the west of them, in fact to the west of the glacier which flows along the base of point 21,747 feet; but I am not nearly so confident on this point as with regard to the views put forward in the preceding paragraph.

It will be gathered from the foregoing observations that the whole of this region would richly repay further exploration. It would provide plenty of mountaineering as well; the northern peaks alone would keep the most strenuous of climbers busy for weeks, and a more charming spot for headquarters could hardly be imagined. Looking back in the light of subsequent happenings, it is difficult to stifle a regret that we did not linger there a little, but we were not prepared for a stay of any length. Moreover, Kamet still beckoned us on like a will-o'-the-wisp; and we still were counting on another campaign, with uninterrupted fine weather and plenty of time, in the upper regions of the Mana valley.

# CHAPTER XIV

## THE MANA VALLEY

STARTING again in beautiful weather on July 14, a forty minutes' scramble up a steep pitch by the side of a prettily wooded cascade brought us to a broad gently-sloping glen, filled with half-withered grass and fields of old snow; then some rather steeper grass slopes led up to a quite considerable snow-field, on the far side of which was the col. As we ascended these, another fine glacier revealed itself among the crags of the northern ridge, the whole length of which was now visible, dominated at the far end by peak 21,191, with which we had grown familiar at Eri Udiar. The panorama extended to peak 21,747, but no farther than that unfortunately, for clouds obstructed the view, so that none of the photographs taken on this day's ascent give any further assistance in locating the puzzling white peak so often referred to. Clouds interfered, too, with the prospect to the west, but for some minutes the wonderful snowy spike of Nilakanta (21,718 feet), the nearest of the Badrinath peaks, could be seen glittering above them. The pass, known to the natives as Khanta Khal, is about 14,500 feet high; we reached it in four hours' walking, the descent taking three more. The narrow glen through which the Mana pass road is reached falls away below it with extraordinary rapidity, descending 6000 feet in two and a half miles; no consideration would induce me to face the crossing of this pass in the reverse direction. There was some fair glissading for some distance below the pass on beds of avalanche snow, which extend almost to the mouth of the glen, where stands the village of Hunuman Chatti. It is a small collection of stone hovels roofed with dried grass, so dirty that we took the precaution of camping a good quarter of a mile away; but a native rest-house, a shop with a large display of eatables and yaks' tails and other local fal-lals, and a holy man with a variety of articles of a religious character for sale, indicated that we had reached the great pilgrims' route.

Beyond Hunuman Chatti the road, here a very fair one, goes through a mere gorge, wild but unattractive; but the walk was full of interest, provided by the ceaseless stream of all sorts and conditions of pilgrims, old and young, rich and poor, of both sexes, from every part of India, on their way to or from Badrinath. Women and portly men of means were being carried in dhoolies by several bearers; old women who could not afford such luxury, and whose size permitted it, were sitting, with their backs turned to the way they were going, in baskets, each slung over the shoulders of a single sturdy carrier; and at least one old man used this mode of conveyance, but the great majority were on foot, many of them, poor souls! hobbling along painfully and very very slowly, for the going was rough in places, and to numbers of the folk from the plains the rocks and stones of a mountain track must have been a novel and excruciating experience. I observed their demeanour towards us to see if I could draw any general inference from it, but without much result. A few salaamed, still fewer showed a scowl of open hostility, but nearly all passed us by with utter indifference and listlessness—the listlessness of fatigue.

Gradually the valley opened out into far the most extensive level tract that we had seen since crossing the Pindar river, and after three hours' easy walking we reached Badrinath, and made our way through the bazaar to the famous temple. Being of no great height, and hemmed in between houses and the steep river-bank, it cannot be seen till one is close to it; but the façade and entrance, which are adorned with some remarkable carvings, are picturesque and not unimpressive, and a little trouble and expense might easily restore it to a state not unworthy of its reputation. It has, however, been suffered to fall into a condition of squalid disorder and disrepair, and evidently it does not form part of the policy of the authorities to spend much of their income, which must be substantial, on its upkeep. No doubt this is partly due to the fact that it is left to itself for half the year to endure the rigours of winter. The whole staff and other inhabitants of the place descend to Joshimath at the end of October, and do not return till May.

To us it was extremely convenient to find a place with a large revenue, as we were able to change any quantity of rupee notes for coin. While Bruce was seeing to this piece of business I watched the pilgrims bathing in the waters of a hot spring which gushes from the rocky bank below, and had a long conversation with the clerk of the temple, who spoke English fluently. He told me that sixty or seventy thousand pilgrims came

there annually from all parts of India; then his face lit up with satisfaction, as he saw his way to making a point, and he went on, "Yes, from all parts of the *world*; *you* are from Europe, and you are here."

Having been decked with garlands, we retraced our steps to the left bank of the river, and tiffined at the dak bungalow, from which there is a splendid view of

Nilakanta, an icy cone of most formidable appearance. The plain extends above Badrinath for quite two miles. At the end of it is Mana, the highest inhabited village, opposite which the plain is joined from the west by a broad side valley leading to the Bagaṭ Kharak and Satopanth glaciers; a fine range of jagged mountain bounds this valley on the north, and, coming right up to the river, appears to block completely the main valley beyond Mana.

We camped a few hundred yards beyond the village just at the base of this seeming *cul de sac*, on the skirts of an astonishing collection of gigantic boulders.

Next day (July 16) I threaded my way through this labyrinth in order to discover by what manner of passage the river makes its way down. At the mouth of the gorge I found a second village overhanging the river, and built in most fantastic and picturesque fashion amongst and over the boulders. The gorge itself is an extraordinary place, reminding one of that of the Tamina at Pfäffers, though on a much smaller scale. The water falls through deep recesses, which even the mid-day sun can scarcely reach, and then descends in a channel so narrow that it is bridged by blocks of stone in four places within a distance of 150-200 yards. The lowest of these natural bridges, slightly assisted by art, provides the regular way of getting across the river from the upper village.

In the meantime Longstaff and the Brocherels went up a hill between Badrinath and the western lateral valley, crowned by a large flagstaff (Pariapal, 14,126 feet), and on their return long and inconclusive dis-

THE GORGE, MANA.

cussions took place with regard to our plans. The big camp was still on its way round from Gamsali, and was not due till the 19th, but we were within easy reach of all necessaries. Of fuel, though not abundance, there was sufficiency, and supplies of tea, rice, dahl, and sugar could be got at the Badrinath bazaar, which contains numerous shops, and even boasts a bookseller.

There had been talk of an expedition up the Bagat Kharak glacier, but Longstaff, having inspected it from the flagstaff hill, threw cold water on this scheme; on the other hand, he had observed an attractive-looking snow-peak on our side of the valley which would provide a climb, and possibly an instructive view towards Kamet, and this was finally decided upon. I was advised to stand out, and collect all my energies for some great effort later on, and I fell in with the suggestion with deplorable readiness. Coolies were engaged to carry up tents, etc.; no doubt, if the following morning had been clear the others would have been off early, but the hillsides were wrapped in a dense mist, and as it was absolutely essential that they should be able to see where they were going, 9.30 found us still all together at breakfast, and, without any formal abandonment of the plan, discussion recommenced. Bruce was not easy in his mind with regard to fuel, and wanted to send some coolies up at once with a store of it towards the Mana pass; indeed, he wanted to go with them, but it was also highly desirable that he should be on the spot when the big camp arrived; the proposed expedition fell into the background, and various alternative ways of dealing with the situation had been put forward and condemned as impracticable, when some one proposed that he should stay behind, and that Longstaff and the Brocherels should go on with the coolies and do some reconnoitring Kamet-wards if possible, while the rest were to follow on the 20th. This satisfied everybody, especially the Brocherels, who were chafing at the prospect of a wasted day; the coolies were already on hand, and they set off before eleven o'clock for Ghastoli, the first of the Bhotia camping-places on the way to the Mana pass, taking with them Dhan Lal and Kul Bahadur.

On the 18th, while Bruce and some of the other Gurkhas climbed the slopes behind Mana in the direction of the abandoned peak of yesterday, Inderbinen and I visited the Bagat Kharak and Satopanth glaciers, which unite close to their termination. We passed on the way an insignificant little shrine at the foot of the northern cliffs, close to a fine waterfall, which is still sought by the more thorough-going of the pilgrims, and commands a view of the snout of the glacier, from which flows the sacred river. In this connection, the following point of local nomenclature is worth recording: the river which descends this valley is called the Alaknanda, both locally and on the maps, but below Mana, where it enters the Sarsuti, the river coming from the Mana pass, their united streams figure on the maps as the Vishnu as far as the junction with the Dhauli, when the name of Alaknanda is revived; we were, however, informed by the patwari of Mana village that this is all wrong: the name of Alaknanda should be preserved throughout; he also stated that Dhauli is a coarse name for the other river, and that *it* should properly be called the Vishnu. It is a great pity that the local method of naming at least the rivers in the Mana valley, which Longstaff has followed in his map, has not been officially adopted; it is far simpler, and serves to emphasise the interesting fact that the two head-streams of the Ganges take their rise in glaciers which are immediately adjacent to each other on opposite sides of the range of the Badrinath peaks.

Above the shrine we noticed on the other side of the river a small but flourishing wood—an unexpected sight, for we had hardly seen a tree since leaving Hunuman Chatti. It supplies Mana, and probably Badrinath also, with fuel, and it seems to be the exclusive duty of the women to collect and carry down the bundles of faggots. Higher up still a wild craggy glen opened up to our right, containing a glacier, the stream from which gave us some trouble to cross. Then rounding the end of a grassy moraine, bright with flowers, we entered a charming sheltered nook, where a flock of unusually good-looking sheep were feeding in charge of a youth and a boy. The latter uttered a startled yell, due, as I at first supposed, to alarm at our terrific appearance, but he was really anxious about the behaviour of a most evil-looking dog, whom he promptly collared. A well-intentioned attempt at conversation collapsed ingloriously, and we left them grinning. It was about three hours' walking to this spot; in half an hour more we reached a point on the moraine which commanded the whole Bagat Kharak glacier. There were several good places for camping between the moraine and the cliffs on the north, if we had decided to explore the glacier farther; but

it was a singularly unattractive one, and by far the dirtiest I have ever set eyes on. Not a sign of ice was visible, and it resembled nothing so much as a London street in one of its earlier stages when it is "up" for repairs. The ridge at its head is low, and there would, I think, be no difficulty on this side in effecting a pass to the Gangotri glacier, the source of the rival head-stream of the Ganges, the Bhagirati. After waiting more than half an hour to secure a view of Nilakanta, which rose steeply above the Satopanth glacier, and looked nearly as inaccessible from here as from Badrinath, we crossed just at the junction of the two glaciers and hurried homewards on the right bank of the river, regaining the northern side by a snow bridge some distance lower down.

I have already had occasion to mention these snow bridges, certainly one of the most remarkable features of the country. Nothing impresses upon one so much the stupendous dimensions of the Himalayan snow-fall as the spectacle of largish rivers covered over at midsummer by solid masses of hard snow, many feet in thickness, which completely fill their channels, sometimes for miles together. They often facilitate travel and make ordinary routes shorter and easier; sometimes they themselves constitute the sole available route. There is a pass into Tibet, a little north-west of Mana, which is described in the G.T.S. map in these terms: "Gumrang or winter pass, closed between May and September, the snow bridges being all swept away."

The snow bridge over the upper Alaknanda saved us a long round, but it was past eight o'clock before we arrived in camp, where we found Bruce patiently waiting for us and for dinner: he had reached a summit on the ridge overlooking the nearest lateral valley to the north, but had not been able to make topographical observations of any interest.

The remaining Gurkhas were very anxious that

he should go up the flagstaff hill next day and do it in better time than the Doctor Sahib; but next day was the date on which the big camp was expected, and no time could be spared for such frivolities. It duly arrived, soon after mid-day. Kharbir had been hampered on the way by running short of coin, and a number of coolies who might otherwise have been dispensed with had been obliged to come on to Badrinath, where notes could be changed, before they could be paid off. It was hard on them, as this was the season when they make their annual journey into Tibet. Otherwise all was well, with Kharbir completely cured of his frost-bites and in excellent spirits at being back with us again.

There was plenty to be done, and much correspondence to be got through; for, besides the letters brought by Kharbir, a post came in from Badrinath later on the same afternoon, the 19th (it included a letter for me that had been posted in London on Friday, June 28). Finally it was past 4 P.M. on the 20th before we started for Ghastoli; Bruce cheerfully announced that it was only six miles, and that we should get in, at latest, by half-past seven; and, untaught by several previous experiences, I believed him. Of course it turned out to be a good deal longer than we had reckoned on, but what completely upset all calculations, and nearly landed us in a situation of serious unpleasantness, was that about an hour after we started Bruce was suddenly attacked by a short sharp fit of fever. The bridge near Ghastoli, as we luckily learnt from a goat-herd, was broken, so it was necessary to cross the river, a foaming raging mass of water of an uncannily bilious green colour, by a bridge of avalanche snow, and then to scramble for some distance along rotten banks of earth and stones. Bruce's strength just lasted till this was passed—fortunately, as it was beginning to get dark—and then he very nearly collapsed. However, with the aid of some brandy and plasmon chocolate, he made another start, and we reached the camp about ten.

A messenger was despatched in the morning with a note warning the others that we should certainly be one, and might be two days longer in joining them; though the fever had quite disappeared, Bruce was all aches and pains, and I never really expected that we should get off again in less than two days.

Ghastoli turned out to be an uninteresting maidan broken up into flat plateaux of varying elevation, and very stony, extending above us for a mile or more. The only noteworthy features in the scene were the ends of two huge terminal moraines projecting from side glens, and almost filling up the main valley, which curved and disappeared just beyond them. Longstaff has named the glaciers to which these moraines belong the Khaiam and Ghastoli glaciers. Southwards the peaks above Mana, the scene of the abandoned expedition of the 18th, rose up finely, reminding one a little of the Wetterhorn on the Rosenlaui side; but of these the clouds only permitted occasional and imperfect glimpses. Chilly mists hung about all day, sometimes descending to the floor of the valley, and completely enveloping the camp, and there was a good deal of rain.

Two days of this had a very damping effect on one's general outlook. We were fixed up with provisions for three weeks, and with a reserve of fuel; but it was no weather for high climbing, and the prospect of waiting indefinitely for an improvement in such dreary surroundings was not alluring. I wondered intermittently what it was like higher up, and how Longstaff and the Brocherels were faring. Was it any better there? Such gleams of better things as there were always showed themselves to the north, and if any break should occur in the rains down below, there was just a chance that we might still get a sunny dry spell. At any rate, I wanted to reach the pass, and set one foot on the soil of the forbidden land before turning my face homeward.

That night Bruce entertained me with a thrilling description of the three days' climbing he had had on Nanga Parbat with Mummery's party. What climbing it was! And how little impression they had made on the great mountain at the end of it!

About 9.30 I made a bolt for my tent through the rain, which had been falling hard and steadily all the evening, and was thinking of turning in, when I heard English voices raised in eager talk, and Bruce gave me a hail. Returning, I found Longstaff, soaked and dripping. On receiving our message he had at once left Jagrau, the last stage before the Mana pass is reached, at 2 P.M., with one coolie, expecting to find us at Balbala, the intermediate camping-ground, and not doing so had pushed on in the dark. He said that he had hurried back, first and principally, in order to dissuade

Bruce, in his invalid condition, from going any farther at present; secondarily, to dissuade both of us from going any farther at all. In order to effect the latter object he launched forth into an eloquent and energetic diatribe, to which I cannot do any sort of justice, on the continuously detestable character of the valley above the Ghastoli maidan.

On the 18th he and the Brocherels had traversed from north to south the ridge between the Khaiam and Ghastoli glaciers, getting a good rock-climb on the descent; they reached a summit of over 18,000 feet, from which a short fleeting glimpse of Kamet tempted them to push on to another point and try for a photograph; but when they got there, it had vanished for good—a last appearance and disappearance thoroughly characteristic of that elusive mountain. Longstaff considered that the Khaiam glacier affords much the most likely route up it, but was convinced that in present circumstances it was much too far off for any attempt to reach it to be worth making. They went on to Balbala, six and a half to seven hours of unspeakably bad going, over moraines, loose stones, banks of shingle; from there, five and a half hours of the same kind of thing to Jagrau; and finally in five hours from this, their farthest camp, they reached the Mana pass, which he described as lying across a level glacier very arctic in character, and quite devoid of interest except in so far as all passes are interesting. Balbala peak was practicable, but he was sure that none of the amateurs would get up it without a long rest. Snow had fallen every day, and the grind of getting there had been very severe; he had never suffered from the effects of altitude so much. If he had known what this valley was like he would never have come up it, but would have gone straight down to Joshimath from Hunuman Chatti; he now proposed to have nothing more to do with it, and to send a party up at once to fetch the Brocherels back as quickly as possible.

He was very much in earnest, and his report practically meant that everything was at an end in Garhwal, so far as climbing was concerned.

It was a severe blow to me to have to give up the Mana pass, and the suggestion was made that I should go on at once with Inderbinen and the men told off to fetch the Brocherels, and make a dash for it, though Longstaff strongly advised me against doing so. It was a difficult question to decide: the weather was doubtful to say the least of it, and I confess that I was daunted by the prospect of having to face some possible emergency or trouble with the coolies, with no moral support, save that of Inderbinen, who could say just three words in Hindustani, *bas* and *garm pani*, and in such a matter would not have been able to give me much help. Longstaff was actually heroic enough, in the teeth of his own emphatic convictions, to offer to return with me; but that, of course, was not to be thought of. I deferred making up my mind till next morning, but Inderbinen's extremely lukewarm attitude, and the night-long patter of the rain on the tent, were too much for me, and I decided to abandon my Pisgah-view of Tibet for good and all. It was just as well that I did so.

There was some faint talk next morning of going up one of the rock peaks behind the camp, but no one's heart was in it, and towards mid-day we set out on our return journey. The broken bridge had been rebuilt—after a fashion—and the passage of it, with that strange-looking green water roaring right under one's feet, was a queer and nerve-trying operation. Bruce, whose head was swimming from many doses of quinine, very wisely returned to the crossing by the avalanche snow. Mana was reached after about three and a half hours' walking, and a little later a storm of rain began, which lasted with scarcely a break for over sixty hours. This clinched matters; if hope had lingered in any mind that things might mend, it did not survive the ordeal of the next two days, and nothing further was heard of anything but retreat.

## CHAPTER XV

### FAREWELL TO GARHWAL

Bed was as good a place as anywhere next morning, and at 11.30 we were still at the breakfast-table in the big tent—what a blessing it was that it was there—when in came Alexis and Henri Brocherel, wetter, if possible, than Longstaff had been when he arrived at Ghastoli.

They had had a very rough time: Henri as usual seemed perfectly jolly and comfortable, but Alexis, though he would not own to having felt at all ill, and certainly looked as fit and serene as ever, admitted that he had only slept three hours in the last three nights, while Kul Bahadur and some of the coolies had been suffering from mountain sickness in the most literal sense of the term, and snow had fallen to the depth of ten centimetres; so yesterday, before our messengers arrived, they had, very sensibly, decided on their own responsibility to come down. In his quiet matter-of-fact way Alexis pictured the situation: they had been obliged to haul the coolies out of their tents, and make up the loads; and then to ruthlessly hustle the coolies, who lay down in the snow and refused to move, into starting. Eventually they reached

Balbala. Coming on in the morning they found the snow-crossing below Ghastoli just, and only just, practicable (they were, of course, unaware that the bridge had been repaired); once safely over the river, they had pushed on at full speed, leaving the Gurkhas to bring in the coolies, which they succeeded in doing at about 6.30 P.M.

My diary, for obvious reasons, is unusually detailed at this point, and contains a lengthy account of the discussions which filled those interminable days. For we had come to the parting of the ways. Of the hopes, on which so much of our programme rested, of getting beyond the rains, not a shred remained, and all August and September were still before us. Long before this Bruce had sketched out a scheme on a big scale of a high-level route westward through Kulu to Kashmir and Khagan; it was a most alluring project, but had been dismissed as being "too large an order"; he now revived it in a much modified and more practicable form, and proposed to me to return direct to Almora and the plains, and go on to Kashmir by the ordinary route from Rawal Pindi. I lent a willing ear, though in doing so I felt like a conspirator, for it meant throwing over Longstaff's much cherished plans for completing the topographical survey of the Trisul massif by an exploration of the glaciers on its western and southern sides. But the bed-rock of the matter was that we had both had enough of Garhwal. Bruce had reasons of his own for wishing to shift his quarters to some place within fairly easy reach of Abbottabad, and was glad to have an opportunity, for once, of showing his favourite beat in Khagan to an appreciative companion, while I was very desirous of putting one or two ascents to my credit, and by no means averse from the prospect of a short spell of civilisation before making a fresh start.

The season for high climbing was clearly over, and neither of us had, like Longstaff, a sort of proprietary interest in Trisul. He, after wavering for a little, finally determined to carry through his original programme, and affected, on what I consider wholly inadequate grounds, to treat us as weathercocks, who would be making arrangements for a visit to Darjiling and Kanchenjunga before another week was out.

I felt a pang at the prospect of turning my back on Mana, which was not solely due to the fact that our travels and plans had there come to a somewhat unlooked for and disappointing termination. I had grown fond of the place, and the people amused and interested me. Though much of the joy of existence in camp flows from the consciousness that one is remote from the world, it is pleasant sometimes to come into contact with human life for a change. And there was plenty of life at Mana. A motley crowd of pilgrims was continually passing by on the way to or from the shrine in the Alaknanda valley, among them some fakirs, their faces and naked bodies smeared all over with a grey mixture of grease and ashes—of these, indeed, one soon saw enough, for they were indescribably repulsive. Then there were the children, with bright faces and active limbs, swarming among the boulders, or hanging about the camp in shy curiosity; and there was a pretty constant going backwards and forwards between the two villages.

On two occasions we came into amusing collision with local beliefs and fancies. On his arrival, Dina established his kitchen in a convenient recess in an extra large rock, and a rumour reached us that the spot was the chosen habitation of the local deity. Nothing further was heard on the subject, however, till the second day of the great downfall of rain. On the afternoon of that day Bruce went down to the lower village, and found the whole population gathered in a solemn assemblage, with the object of procuring fair weather. The procedure seems to be that silence prevails till the god enters into one of those present and inspires him to speak. I believe the meeting was partly due to anxiety on account of a party of villagers who were returning over the Mana pass from Tibet. However this may be, it was quite a genuine affair up to this point, for they could not possibly have known that Bruce was coming; but no sooner did he appear than some one was moved to say that the rain was due to the wrath of the god at his abode being invaded ; if, however, the visitors would sacrifice a goat, he would be appeased, and would acquiesce in the intrusion and stop the rain. Bruce replied with due gravity that unfortunately he was unable to comply with this suggestion, as he never sacrificed goats; if he ever did sacrifice anything, it was a camel. No answer was vouchsafed to the next inspired utterance, which was to the effect that in these circumstances the case could be satisfactorily met by a donation of rupees.

It would probably be easy to parallel this; but the other episode is really curious: I give the facts as I learned them, without comment. One morning, before we went to Ghastoli, Jeman Sing, one of the Gurkhas, asked permission of Bruce to take away the water in which he had washed his face and give it to a woman in the village. Bruce said, "Yes, certainly," and remarked that he had rarely been paid such a compliment, whereupon Jeman Sing grinned in such a fashion that he pressed for further particulars. Jeman Sing then explained that, on the previous day, Bruce had come suddenly upon the woman round a corner, and startled her so much that she had gone home and taken to her bed, and was lying there ill.

He had no recollection of the occurrence, but it was very easy indeed to come on people round corners among the big boulders by the camp; in fact, one could hardly move twenty yards without doing so.

Later in the day, being in the village with Kharbir, he was requested to go to the woman's house and see her. She was up and about, and replied to his inquiries that she was now quite well again, thanks to his kindness in sending the water. Asked further what she had done with it, "Oh," she said, "I drank it."

It is to be hoped that any moral or material damage which the inhabitants of Mana suffered from our sojourn in their neighbourhood was more than compensated by the legacy of tins, jam-pots, bottles, etc., which we shed on our departure. Such articles are highly treasured in these valleys, where anything made of glass or china is very rarely seen; and I don't know how we should have got on ourselves without the aid of the large tins of the Standard Oil Company, which were put to all kinds of strange uses, and in particular were indispensable in places where water was only to be obtained by melting snow. "I have always been told," a shikari on the North-West frontier once remarked, "that the English sahibs were very wealthy; and now

I know it."—"How so?"—"Because you throw away your tins."

After devoting a day to drying our belongings—the tents were saturated, and everything was more or less wet—we descended on the 27th to the dak bungalow at Pandukeswar, half-way to Joshimath, a march of about four hours and a quarter. Close to the village stands a Hindu temple, containing some ancient grants of land engraved on copper plates; a *fac-simile* of one is given in Atkinson's *Himalayan Districts*.

A little farther on the river is joined by the Bhyundar torrent, coming down from the glen, whose upper levels we had traversed on June 12 and 13. Between Hunuman Chatti and this point the valley of the Vishnu is fairly open and well wooded; the scenery is always pleasing, and at times beautiful, with the familiar beauty born of rock, brawling waters, and rich vegetation. Here the scene changes: the valley contracts, and the river foams and frets on its way to the Dhauli, six or seven miles below, through a gloomy defile of rare grandeur. I noticed a single palm tree, standing forlorn and solitary by the water's edge, but the dark walls on either hand are mostly bare. The pilgrims' way has needed a good deal of engineering here to render it practicable, and is carried in places high above the river. Tradition says that at one convenient spot pilgrims were not infrequently tipped over the precipice into the river, and their carriers, who had been paid beforehand for the journey to Badrinath and back, returned for another job. The latter defended this proceeding on the ground that death in the cleansing stream itself made their employers' entry into Paradise a certainty, so that they secured the real object of their journey more expeditiously than they had bargained for, and thus every one was benefited; but the practice has become obsolete since the establishment of the unimaginative British raj.

Above the river, as it thunders down into the Dhauli, the few squalid houses of Vishnu Prayag are huddled together on a narrow shelf, from which a staircase, cut in the solid stone, enables pilgrims to descend and immerse themselves at the very meeting-point of the waters—always a place of special sanctity; but it looks a formidable operation, and one is not surprised to read that many are drowned.

The channel of the Dhauli is here even more precipitous and confined than that of the Vishnu; one rounds a sharp angle of naked rock, and goes up-stream for fifty yards or so, along a still narrower shelf to the suspension bridge. It is a wonderful scene; but to get a satisfactory view of it one would need to be suspended in mid-air over the spot where the united streams go roaring down the chasm out of sight. It is just at this point that the two rivers cut through the main axis of the Great Himalayan chain.

A steep ascent of about an hour, mostly by means of rude staircases of stones, brings one out on to the irregular uplands on which stands the town of Joshimath. It turned out to be impossible to push on farther towards the Kuari pass, as had been intended, but I was glad to have an afternoon to spend in wandering through the quaint streets and examining the extremely picturesque temple. The dak bungalow is quite a palatial building, erected, I believe, by the authorities of Badrinath. The patwari paid us a state visit there, bringing a gift of melons, pears, figs, almonds, etc., and a collection of old "chits" of his father's. Two of these were of real interest—one from Colonel Smyth commending his conduct in the course of the passage of a glacier pass in 1867; the other, referring, in a similar sense, to the crossing of Traill's pass, was signed by Adolph Schlagintweit.

On the 29th we rejoined our old route, camping, in

a deluge of rain, on the skirts of the woods above Tapoban, and the following day crossed the Kuari pass to Pana. The pass was transformed out of all recognition: not a trace remained of the snow on which we

had glissaded for hundreds of feet in May; the slopes were covered with luxuriant waving grass, and once more Inderbinen bewailed the fact that there were no cows engaged in converting it into marketable butter and cheese.

At Pana began the unsoldering of our goodly

fellowship. Longstaff remained behind with Dhan Lal and Kul Bahadur. He worked hard for a month among the glaciers round the western and southern bases of Trisul, and obtained a rich harvest of topographical results, which he has recorded in the journals of the Alpine Club and the Geographical Society.[1]

The rest of us returned on our own tracks, and were again hospitably entertained by Mr. and Mrs. Nash at Gwaldam (where we deposited most of our remaining stores, to await Longstaff's arrival), and by the brothers Troupe at Kausani. At Gwaldam, too, we parted with the excellent and invaluable Lachman, and the bulk of the coolies. Most of these latter had only been with us for a march or two. A few farewell words are due to one other faithful companion of most of our travels, Seban Sing, usually known, from one of his many functions, as the tiffin-wallah, but best remembered by me as the bringer of the early morning cup of tea. At high camps and in rough weather this duty was no joke; and from time to time he would point wistfully to his long lean lower limbs, and prefer what I construed to be a request—which I was not in a position to gratify—for an old pair of trousers. Not till near the end, when the worst times were over, did I realise that what he craved was not trousers but stockings, and I hastened to present him with a pair; but I still have remorseful visions of his shivering naked legs at the entrance of the tent on a snowy morning.

On August 6 we were back in Almora once more,

[1] *Alpine Journal*, vol. xxiv. p. 131; *Geographical Journal*, vol. xxxi. p. 386.

and there another parting took place; we had tried hard to persuade the Brocherels to accompany us to Kashmir, but they were obliged to hurry on to Bombay in time to catch the first available boat. Of their professional powers enough has been said already, and better comrades no man could desire; they possess in full measure those qualities which have endeared guides of the best class to many generations of mountaineers, and evoked eulogies from pens whose eloquence I cannot attempt to rival.

Unforeseen circumstances detained us at Almora for nine days. We ought to have chafed at the delay, but our hosts of the 3rd Gurkhas made the time pass so pleasantly, that even now I cannot regret it. On the afternoon of the 15th we left for Peora, using a short-cut, under the guidance of Bruce, whose knowledge of the Himalaya resembles Sam Weller's knowledge of London; and at mid-day on the 17th we reached the bungalow of his brother-in-law, Mr. John Campbell, at Naini Tal.

There I was fortunate enough to enjoy the view—oceanic in its immensity—over the plains, but was prevented by the weather from making the ascent of the local *belvedere*, Cheena, which combines this view with a distant prospect of the snows co-extensive with that obtained from Peora. Of Naini Tal itself I need not speak, for there one falls within the range of Murray's *Handbook to India*. It was one of life's little ironies that here should occur the first and only hitch in Bruce's *bandobast*, which had coped triumphantly with all the difficulties of the wilderness for three months; but so it was. We managed to miss the train at Kathgodam by a quarter of an hour, and thereby lost another day, so that it was not till the evening of the 21st that we arrived at Rawal Pindi, the starting-point for Kashmir.

Before saying a final good-bye to Garhwal I will take the opportunity of making a few general remarks as to my impressions of our journey and of the country, particularly of the country regarded as a mountaineering resort. One of the outstanding features of the journey was that there was so little real climbing; I did practically none; even those members of the party who accomplished most, did very little compared to what they would have done in the Alps in half the time. But it would be a great mistake to argue that this was because there was not enough to do; it would be much nearer the truth to say that it was because there was a great deal too much. Garhwal is not a good place for breaking altitude records, but, subject to that qualification, it is embarrassingly rich in mountaineering possibilities, far more so than we had realised beforehand.

It is easy now to see how, at one stage or another, we might have ordered things differently and turned our opportunities to better account, but it was not easy at the time. The true lessons to be drawn from our experiences are that the higher parts of the Mana and Niti valleys are not the best but the very worst places to be in when the rains arrive, and that it was a mistake to try to cover all the ground and combine Nanda Devi and Kamet in a single season.

I should go even further than this, and advise the next Garhwal party—if they find the magnetism of Nanda Devi irresistible—to make up their minds to spend the whole season in the Rishi valley. The discovery of a key which will unlock the entrance to the Nanda Devi basin, the ascents of Dunagiri and Changabang, and the solution of the problems connected with Graham's doings, will provide an ample and varied bill of fare.

As the best alternative to this, I should recommend them to harden their hearts and, leaving both Kamet and Nanda Devi severely alone, to devote themselves exclusively to the mountains lying to the south of the Raikana glacier. That is what I should do myself if I was ever in the Dhauli valley again. Persons addicted to mountaineering resemble the immortal Mr. Woodhouse, who liked his gruel to be thin, but not too thin; they like their climbing to be difficult, but not too difficult, and the whole of Alpine history for the last fifty years is but a development of that simple statement. I believe that the last-mentioned district would provide as near an approximation to the golden mean as can be found in the Himalaya, or elsewhere; there are many topographical questions waiting to be cleared up, and a large number of peaks to be climbed. Few of them will turn out to be easy, but neither heights nor distances are unmanageably huge.

When I left home, the two things about which I felt anxious were mountain-sickness and cold. The completeness with which cold can be defied, as long as one stays inside a Mummery tent and a sleeping-bag, was an agreeable surprise; but mountain-sickness is a drawback which cannot be denied or got rid of. I do not think any healthy person need trouble himself greatly about the acuter forms of attack; they may come or they may not, but at the worst they are soon over—in a few days at most. But in its more insidious form of mountain lassitude it is always with one more or less, undermining one's energy, and leading one to take things easily to an extent which one regrets when it is too late. I have come to one very decided conclusion about it, namely, that its effects are more severely felt as one grows older. Our party offered excellent material for observations on this point, as the ages of its members ranged from about thirty to fifty-one. The Brocherels, it is true, seemed to be entirely immune; but of the rest of us, I think there is no doubt that Bruce felt it distinctly more than Longstaff, and that Inderbinen and I, whose symptoms generally moved in melancholy parallels, felt it most of all. The crucial case is that of Inderbinen. He is still, like most guides who have taken proper care of themselves, going nearly as well as he ever did in the Alps; but he was undoubtedly the greatest sufferer, and on at least two occasions—on the Bagini glacier and later on the final slope of Haramukh—found difficulty in breathing under conditions where I, though not exactly yearning to go faster, was in that respect perfectly comfortable.

The weather during May and the first half of June was by no means so good as I had been led to expect;

few days were altogether fine—unbroken spells of several such days in succession hardly occurred at all, and the longest did not exceed five or six days. On the other hand, the mornings, till mid-day or thereabouts, were clear and sunny almost without exception, and the storms of snow or rain, which usually began at two or three in the afternoon, rarely lasted much more than a couple of hours; I can recall very few occasions when we could not enjoy a comfortable smoke by the fire, under a quiet starlit sky, before turning in. One is tempted to assume that these weather conditions are a normal type to which all seasons approximate; perhaps it is rash to take so much for granted, but I should be much surprised to learn that the seasons vary to anything like the extent to which the Alps have accustomed us.

I have nothing instructive to add with regard to matters of *bandobast*. Our caravan was managed with such foresight and generalship that none of those mishaps befel us which serve to others for edification and warning. It would be impossible to overstate the debt of gratitude which Longstaff and I owe to Bruce for his unflagging and self-effacing exertions, and the one untoward event in our tour was the deplorable indisposition which prevented him from reaching the summit of Trisul.

The Bridge, Kairen.

## CHAPTER XVI

### KASHMIR AND HARAMUKH

WHEN the move from Garhwal to Kashmir was decided upon, I was invited by Bruce to regard it in the same light as exchanging the eastern for the western Alps. It is an apt and suggestive analogy in many ways: the relation in height between the Garhwal peaks and those in the immediate neighbourhood of the vale of Kashmir, none of which much exceed 17,000 feet, is roughly proportionate to that of the Pennine summits to those of Tyrol; and with this diminution in size, the value of the valley scenery increases, and the attractiveness of the landscape no longer depends principally on the grandeur and variety of the mountain forms above the snow-line. But neither the views nor the climbing in Kashmir have any resemblance to those provided by the Dolomites: from the climbing point of view our trip was more like a visit to such outlying ranges as that of the Glärnisch; as regards scenery, the comparison which suggested itself to me was not Tyrolese, but Italian, and you get a very fair idea of what the vale of Kashmir is like by imagining the Alps to be bent round so as to enclose an oval piece of the Piedmontese plain with a general north-west and south-easterly direction, about eighty miles in length by twenty miles broad.

The river Jhelam, which drains the vale, flows placidly and sedately across its levels to Baramula, where, plunging into the mountains through a narrow gap, it becomes a roaring raging torrent, which flows westward for nearly eighty miles to Mozufferabad, then turns south down a tremendous defile towards the plains. Driving up from Rawal Pindi the traveller has to make a steep ascent to the well-known hill station of Mari (where I was providentially able to replenish my stock of photographic plates), and then drops rapidly into this defile, reaching the river at Kohala, about twenty miles below the southern bend. Here begins the famous "Jhelam Valley Road," completed about eighteen years ago, and here are the remains of the old suspension bridge which was carried away by a flood in 1898. The river, when I saw it at this point, was sliding smoothly along, far below the level of its precipitous rocky banks, and the narrowness of the channel was really astounding. Not that there is anything very remarkable to the eye, but when one sees the stream in its earlier stages, at Baramula and Srinagar, it seems almost inconceivable that it could be pent up in so small a space, though the volume of water at Kohala is far greater than when it leaves the vale; the depth of the channel must be prodigious.

Close to its southward turn the Jhelam is joined from the north, within a distance of five or six miles, by two considerable tributaries—the Kunhar or Nainsook, which flows through the valley of Khagan, and the Kishenganga, a river which plays a very important part in the orography of Kashmir. They are separated by a fine range of snowy mountains, which does not seem to have any recognised designation, and I shall follow Bruce in referring to it as the Khagan range. No one has so good a right as he to christen it; the surveyors have left their mark on it, but I believe that no one except him and some of his Gurkhas has really explored that portion of it which rises above the snow-line.

"One way," says Mr. F. Drew, "of looking at the mountains that make the oval barrier of Kashmir, is to consider them as divided into a northern and a southern part by the Sind river that flows from near the Dras pass (now more commonly known as the Zoji La) into the vale, and the Jhelam river as it flows out from Baramula to Muzufarabad [where it is joined by the Kishenganga]. The line of these two is roughly east and west; it divides the vale and its mountain-ring into somewhat unequal parts, of which the southern is the greater.

"The northern part extends for over a hundred miles from east to west. . . . On its south side lie successively the Sind valley, the northern part of the vale, and the Jhelam valley; on the north side is the Kishenganga valley in its whole length."[1]

This way of looking at it is extremely convenient for the purpose of giving a brief outline of our trip, the general idea of which was to follow the imaginary dividing line for most of its length, and on the return

[1] *Jummoo and Kashmir Territories*, p. 199.

journey first to see something of the spurs and valleys of the northern part of the mountain-ring as above described, and to attempt the ascent of Haramukh, its one big peak; then to follow the Khagan range to its southern extremity, thus making a sort of high-level circular tour round the northern half of the vale.

I need not linger over the drive from Rawal Pindi to Kashmir, which is now accomplished by hundreds of persons annually, and has been most vividly described by Mr. E. F. Knight in that most fascinating book, *Where Three Empires Meet*. When he went up the Jhelam valley in 1891 the journey from Baramula onward was completed by boat, but the road now runs all the way to Srinagar. The tradition of furious driving has been faithfully preserved, and the whole distance of 196 miles from Rawal Pindi is sometimes covered in two days when the road is clear; we accomplished it easily in three, our progress being a good deal hampered by processions of bullock-carts, heavily laden with apples and walnuts, and much too large for the roadway, of which we must have passed some hundreds. The amount of traffic turned one's thoughts to railways, and a railway to Srinagar has been discussed for some time past, but so far as I am aware it still remains in the region of discussion. I should imagine that the engineering difficulties would be considerable, as the walls of the valley are composed of exceedingly rotten rock, and small land-slides and rock-falls are of frequent occurrence; we passed several gangs of workmen engaged in repairing damage due to this cause. However, railway or no railway, Kashmir has already become, if not an Indian Switzerland, at any rate the playground of India; three guide-books at least have been devoted to it, one of them adorned with flowery extracts from "Lalla Rookh," which recall the quotations from Byron in earlier editions of "Murray," and incidentally make one open one's eyes at the poetical taste of our great-grandparents.

And the Kashmiris display in a very marked manner the characteristics of a people with whom the exploitation of globe-trotters has become a regular business. They are a fine-looking race, well clothed and with every sign of well-being about them—very different from the poorly-nourished and poorly-clad Garhwalis; but they have the unenviable reputation of being exceptionally cowardly: I once saw one collapse into a sitting posture in the middle of a road and display every sign of abject fear at the yapping and snapping of a very insignificant cur, and was told that his behaviour was typical and characteristic. It certainly was an ignoble spectacle, but I think the attitude of most people towards even a small dog would be considerably modified if their feet and legs were bare. Their eagerness to get as much as possible out of visitors is not a particularly engaging trait; but it makes for comfort—and the conditions of travel generally in Kashmir, as compared with Garhwal, are more than comfortable, they are luxurious.

Srinagar at the end of August was still very hot, and practically empty of European visitors. We spent three days there, during which I raced up the Takht-i-Suleiman with Inderbinen (and was absurdly pleased afterwards when I learned that Jeman Sing, who accompanied us, had reported to Bruce that the Sahib had done it in very quick time), went for a row on the Dal lake, shopped extravagantly, and generally enjoyed such diversions as Srinagar has to offer out of the season. Late in the afternoon of August 27 we started for our first objective, Mount Haramukh, a huge isolated mass, whose snowy crest is visible from Srinagar towering nearly 12,000 feet above the vale, and though only 16,904 feet above sea-level, overtopping by thousands of feet everything in its immediate neighbourhood.

The history of Haramukh has been briefly told in the *Alpine Journal*[1] by Dr. E. F. Neve. One of its outlying western peaks, known as "Station Peak" (about 16,000 feet), was visited many years ago by the surveyors, but no attempt on the main mountain was made till much later. Dr. Neve, after several visits, for the first time attained a point on the principal ridge in 1897, and finally reached the highest summit with Mr. Geoffrey Millais in 1899. Whether he or any one else has repeated the expedition since, I do not know; however, our natural wish, as a first ascent was not open to us, was to discover a new route and, if possible, to make a traverse of the mountain. A visit to Kashmir and Khagan had formed no part of our original plans, and consequently we had taken no steps to provide ourselves with maps, or to acquire any information about the topography of Haramukh. Probably any efforts in this direction would have been useless, as I

[1] Vol. xx. p. 122.

have since failed to discover any maps of Kashmir on a scale which would be of any value for mountaineering purposes. The Government map published in 1867 on a scale of five miles to an inch gives an excellent general idea of the country, but the mountains are represented in the conventional caterpillar style, and there is no attempt at accuracy in detail. Fortunately, however, during our short stay at Srinagar we met Dr. Neve and his brother, who are resident physicians at the Kashmir State Hospital; they supplied Bruce with a rough but serviceable sketch-map, and much useful information.

Haramukh does not form part of any main watershed: it is an outlier of the northern mountain-ring situated between two nearly parallel valleys, the Erin nala and the Wangat nala, which descend to the vale of Kashmir in a south-westerly direction. The former, the more northerly of the two, runs right down to the great Wular lake; the latter joins the larger valley of the Sind river a short distance before it debouches into the plain. They are connected by a fairly good track running round the mountain on the north-west and north, and leading over two low passes.

We left Srinagar in two doongas, or native house-boats, and dropped down-stream to Shadipore. Thither the Sind river meanders through the flat country to join the Jhelam by half a dozen different channels, and in the mists of next morning we might have fancied ourselves on the Norfolk Broads. Gradually the mountains were unveiled, and, amid scenes of ever-increasing beauty, the voyage came to an end at Gunderbal, near the mouth of the Sind valley.

Travelling in a doonga is a delectable method of locomotion, especially when it is not the dwelling-place of the wife and children of the owner, as is usually the case. The owner of ours, Ahadoo by name, struck me as being a representative Kashmiri of the type indicated above—an unctuous voluble ruffian, whom one could imagine being truculent under favourable circumstances. He left me no peace till I had read all his chits or testimonials. It is rash to make any generalisation about the inhabitants of the Indian peninsula, but one may safely say that any possessor of a chit from an Englishman is consumed by a perpetual and passionate desire to get other Englishmen to read it, quite regardless of its tenor. Ahadoo's employers had one and all dwelt, as I did in due course before we parted, on the advantage of the fact that he did not bring his family with him; one of them had added a short sketch of him which is worth preserving: "Morals I imagine he has none, but if he had they would be doubtful." But he was amusing in short spells. I asked him something about a party who were at Gunderbal in a large house-boat of the kind one sees at such places as Henley; he misinterpreted the question as a general one about the pursuits and objects of visitors to Kashmir, and had his classification ready: "Some Sahib shootin' shikar; some Sahib fishin' shikar; some Sahib sit down—sle-e-e-p."

I walked over in the afternoon through rice and

maize fields, dotted with chenars, willows, and poplars, to the pretty little Manasbal lake, at the foot of one of the Haramukh spurs. On the following morning a post arrived with a telegram, which, to the great regret of every one, summoned Kharbir back to Abbottabad. We left him to return with the doongas,

and proceeded along the route used by pilgrims on the outward journey to the sacred Gungabal lake, camping on August 30 close to the ruins of the Wangat temples. These mysterious remains, curiously remote in character from all other types of Indian architecture, are similar in character and origin to the larger and better known ruins of Martand. Sir Martin Conway turned aside to visit them on his way back from Leh in 1892, and has described them and their surroundings at some length in his *Climbing and Exploration in the Karakoram Himalayas.* A short distance above the ruins the Wangat valley branches to the right and left. Ascending by the steep zigzags of the pilgrims' route, we came suddenly round a corner, facing up the left-hand branch, and had our first view of the eastern face of Haramukh, an imposing but monotonous wall of dark rock, with one huge shelf, over which sprawled a considerable glacier. The next day was devoted to photography and a careful examination of possible routes, and the camp was moved up to the banks of the Gungabal lake, which skirts the base of Haramukh up to the head of this branch of the Wangat valley.

Dr. Neve had told us that we should find the east face rather a hard nut to crack, and suggested that a much likelier route would be provided by a glacier on the other side of the northern end of the mountain, the final ice-fall of which, dropping steeply to the shore of the upper end of the lake, was visible from the camp. The east face is certainly the "wrong side" of Haramukh, in the sense that it offers the most difficult and doubtful route, and the best climbing. Whether that is equivalent to saying that it is the most attractive route depends on one's point of view at the moment. We wanted to make sure of the peak, and could not afford to spend much time on it; accordingly, the camp being now in a commanding position with respect to the east face, we determined to have a look at the route indicated by Dr. Neve before coming to a final decision.

On Monday, September 2, we started with Pahal

Sing and Jeman Sing, walked briskly along the lake, and arrived in an hour at the far end of it, beyond the glacier. Another hour's steady going up steep grass slopes along the left side of the glacier brought us to a point above the icefall, from which we could see right up the glacier to the snowy cirque at its head, and the route now looked so promising that Jeman Sing was

forthwith sent back with instructions to return to the same place with a sufficiency of tents and provisions and pitch a camp there.

The four who were left took to the ice, went on for an hour, and then put on crampons at the foot of the second icefall. These were practically a novelty to all the party, and we could not possibly have had a better occasion for making acquaintance with them. The slopes were mostly of hard ice, just a little too steep to walk up without step-cutting in ordinary foot-gear, and it was a very pleasing experience to find oneself marching up them with perfect comfort and ease. The crevasses were magnificent and on a large scale, but presented no difficulties, and the only feature of this portion of the ascent which calls for any remark was an ugly-looking bit of glacier at the top of the cliffs on our left, just where the crevasses came to an end, and the plateau of névé commenced which forms the source of the glacier. We kept a wary eye on it, but nothing came down.

We were now in a position to grasp more clearly the structure of the mountain. In front of us a snowy ridge descended in a north-westerly direction from the main mass, and, curving round to the north, was continued in an irregular series of cliffs and small rock-peaks, which formed the western boundary of the Gungabal glacier, and, sinking still lower, closed the valley at the head of the Gungabal lake, and connected the outlying Haramukh massif with the watershed between the basins of the Sind river and the Kishenganga.

The plateau, rising gently, brought us to a snowy col at the point where the ridge turns to the north. We conjectured, quite correctly, that at this point or near it we must join Dr. Neve's route, and hoped to be able to form some notion of the way by which he had come; but everything on the other side was shrouded in dense mist, and it was impossible to do so. A convenient snow-terrace provided easy going for some distance farther, and then only a short scramble remained between us and a snowy dome on the main ridge, which clearly overtopped everything in sight to the north. For a few minutes we believed that we had the top "in our pocket," but when the dome was reached another dome loomed up through the clouds beyond it, which very palpably looked down on us. We had, in fact, reached the "middle dome" ascended by Dr. Neve in 1897, and between us and the highest peak yawned the deep gap which he did not cross till two years later. Half filled by rolling mists, it looked quite formidable. It was now past two o'clock; we were desperately hungry, and one of us, at any rate, was tired. There was no chance of a view, so at three it was decided to return and complete the ascent another day.

We had just crossed the plateau and rounded the first of the big crevasses, when the overhanging glacier had a shot at us; it was just too late, and one or two big lumps that would have reached us disappeared harmlessly into the depths of the crevasse. Had they come a minute sooner we should have had to make a bolt for it, but there would have been time. Soon afterwards the tents came in sight, and we were back before five.

On September 4, after a wholly inexcusable and wholly pleasant day of idleness, we started at 7.40; going steadily, and at a good pace, I reached the middle dome at eleven with Inderbinen and Pahal Sing; Bruce, Jeman Sing, and Ranbir had left the ridge lower down to try a direct traverse to the gap.

We got down to the gap in half an hour, by rocks which, though steep and rotten, turned out to be quite easy, and strolled in another half-hour up the broad snow arête that led to the summit. Bruce's division were let in for a difficult descent, which landed them some way below the gap, and we were nearly an hour on the top before they joined us. The way over the middle dome is decidedly the best and shortest.

"The scene was too grand for words to describe. One looked right over the top of the great Pir Panjal range, which lies to the south of the valley of Kashmir, and the higher peaks of which rival and even surpass Mont Blanc in height. Looking around one saw, standing out like giants, the still unclimbed mountains —Kolahoi, with its Matterhorn-like peak; Nun Kun; to the north, Gwasherbrum and Masherbrum; and above all, sixty miles away, the grand range culminating in Nanga Parbat."

So Dr. Neve ends the story of his first ascent: of this unsurpassable panorama we saw nothing. Looking back dispassionately on our whole journey, I think we had at least average good luck in this respect; to have wholly missed the view from Haramukh was the one supreme unforgettable disappointment.

But Haramukh is far too fine a mountain to be dismissed as a mere *belvedere*. It is the giant of the northern mountain-ring, which elsewhere scarcely reaches the snow-line. The ice scenery is of a high order, and the ascent, though easy, is well worth making for its own sake. And there is the east face climb waiting for the next comer. The point to make for is the gap, and I should not be surprised if the last few hundred feet turned out to be decidedly interesting. A party who succeeded in reaching the summit from this side could fairly reckon on regaining a camp at the bottom of the Gungabal lake by our route in four or five hours. We got back to the middle dome in three-quarters

of an hour, the leading trio going slowly up the rocks for fear of sending stones down. On the rest of the descent we went very fast over the now familiar ground, and reached the camp by the glacier in an hour and twenty-five minutes.

Unfortunately, the remarkably isolated position of Haramukh, to which its interest is largely due, is also the cause of its being neglected. The tour of the mountain from Srinagar to the Wular lake occupies eight or ten days, and mountaineering parties coming from distant lands, and intent on more distant and bigger game, will rarely pause to devote so much time to it. Even Bruce had never before found time

for a visit, and its exploration so far has been left altogether to residents in Srinagar.

On September 5 we took a short-cut across the Gungabal ridge just behind the camp, skirted the curious little Sirbal lake, and then, crossing a second low col, dropped down a very steep descent to a charming maidan at the very head of the Erin nala. This day was our last chance of seeing something of the western flanks of Haramukh; unluckily it was very cloudy, and I could not get any idea of the route by which the earlier ascents were made.

Down the densely-wooded Erin nala, through typical Kashmiri scenery, luxuriant vegetation, pretty prosperous-looking villages half-buried in trees, sparkling streams and bright-green meadows, we emerged on the 7th into the dust and glare of the open plain at Bandipore, an important place, the starting-point for two passes, the Tragbal and the Borzil, which lead into and out of the Kishenganga valley, and so into the basin of the Indus and on to Gilgit and Hunza. A short mile away was the Wular lake, where Ahadoo and the doongas were waiting for us. Haramukh has an unfair advantage over all other mountains in that the natural sequel to an ascent of it is a spell of idling in a doonga. As, next day, we dawdled across the lake to Alsoo, I thought that for once in my mountaineering life I was touching the heights of perfect achievement—I was having the ideal off-day. But there were drawbacks: the temperature of the water was delicious, but the weeds were so thick and so near the surface that a swim would have been risky, and all that was possible in the way of a bathe was to dangle in the water, hanging on cautiously to the edge of the vessel. And at Alsoo my ideal day was brought to an ignominious close by countless myriads of mosquitoes, which drove us to a gobbled dinner, hurried packing, and a flight shorewards through a hundred yards of sludge to comparative safety at the top of a neighbouring knoll.

# CHAPTER XVII

## KHAGAN AND SHIKARA

FROM Alsoo we made a fresh start: twenty-five stalwart Kashmiri porters had been engaged to come with us right through to Abbottabad, our ultimate bourne; and a store of provisions for about a fortnight had been sent by water from Srinagar to meet us. It had been arranged some time previously that Dina, who had gone straight back to Abbottabad, should come up with mules and fresh supplies, and meet us in the Safa Mula valley, on the far side of the Khagan range.

Just to the north of the Wular lake, a spur sweeps down into the vale from its mountain-ring and encloses the lovely valley of the Lolab. Camping on the neck, on a delightful greensward girdled with pine woods, I wandered forth in the early morning with Inderbinen and a camera, hoping for a long shot at Haramukh. Haramukh was coyly veiled in haze, but away to the north, through the trees, we spied some snowy peaks hitherto unseen, and moved a little to get an unimpeded look at them; then as our eyes travelled on from one to the other, they were suddenly arrested by a white monster, which dwarfed the other summits into puny insignificance; and so, by the merest chance, I obtained my one and only view of Nanga Parbat.

It is an event in a lifetime merely to have gazed on that superb and stupendous mountain, by far the loftiest in the Western Himalaya, and surpassed in height by K 2 only among the giants of the Karakoram. And, unlike them, and the still more gigantic peaks in the

East, Nanga Parbat stands alone, overtopping all other summits within 120 miles by more than 9000 feet. Due homage is paid to it in Kashmir; on the maps in the guide-books one finds indicated the places on the road to Srinagar from which it may be seen in clear weather; and in the post-office at Bandipore we met a member of a party which was just starting on an expedition of several days' duration, with the sole object of getting a nearer view of it from the Borzil pass. I had for a short time cherished the hope that it might be possible for us to go round Nanga Parbat on the north, and see it rising more than 23,000 feet above the Indus valley—the greatest mountain view in the world; but this idea had been long ago abandoned. The next few days' walking was flat and uneventful; the nearest approach to anything exciting was that a bear paid a visit to the camp one night, but the Gurkhas shoo'ed it away, and we knew nothing of the episode till next morning. We went down the Lolab, unrivalled even in Kashmir for sumptuous and exuberant fertility, skirted the northern edge of the vale, spending one pleasant afternoon under the fine trees which surround the sacred fish-ponds of Tregam, and on September 18 crossed Drew's northern ring by the Patu Khar pass, descending through magnificent forests to the Kishenganga at Kairen, where it is spanned by a quaint old bridge, with a very solid stone building at one end of it, originally, no doubt, erected for military purposes.

We were not yet, however, in touch with the Khagan range—a tributary glen intervened, that of the Jagran river, which flows for a long distance nearly parallel with the Kishenganga before joining it; the upper level of this glen, an extensive pasture-ground, is known as Tod Galli, and is reached from the Kishenganga by the Babun pass. The map of 1867 has the name Tor Galli, but knows nothing of a Babun pass; I give these names on the authority of Bruce, who impressed upon me that "Toad gully" and "Baboon pass" were particularly easy to remember. This route seems to be the quickest and most direct way of reaching the Khagan mountains from the side of Kashmir, and it is full of interest and variety. From the edge of the vale to Tod Galli is three good days' walking. The splendid forests of the Patu Khar pass constitute the principal feature of the first day; on the second, the exquisite valley scenery of the Kishenganga about and above the Kairen bridge. From the Babun pass itself

the view to the east is panoramic; we gazed across an endless sea of wooded ranges, above which rose Haramukh, a massive island of rock. This was our last clear sight of it, and we realised once more, with a pang of regret, its unrivalled position as a view point. On the west, now close at hand, were some of the numerous Rajee Bojee peaks, which are situated in the southern half of the snowy portion of the Khagan range, and have been the principal scene of Bruce's activities; right in front of us was one which Harkir, one of his companions on Pioneer Peak, climbed alone in 1896.[1]

A steep descent, which recalled bits of the Rishi valley, landed us on September 15 in Tod Galli, at the lower end of a wide-spreading maidan.

One could see up the valley for perhaps three or four miles, then it turned sharply to the left, and was

lost to view behind a sturdy rock peak. As we were going up the other side, two days later, an attractive-looking glacier pass came into view, just opposite the corner, which must lead back into the Kishenganga basin, and invites further investigation. Bruce knew nothing of this upper region of the valley, and doubted whether any one had ever visited it.

[1] *Alpine Journal*, vol. xx. pp. 306-310.

Eleven years before, he and his party, having descended into Tod Galli on the occasion of Harkir's solitary ascent, returned "over a couple of passes and an elevated snow-field which took them down into the Narang valley of Khagan," and this route he proposed to follow once more. It would bring us into the neighbourhood of Mali (17,346 feet), the giant of the chain, and Shikara; we hoped to climb these two peaks, and then to work our way through the lateral valleys on the north side of the chain by a series of subalpine passes.

On September 17 we walked to the upper end of the maidan, crossed the river, not without difficulty, near some herdsmen's huts—the highest human habitations—and then, ascending steeply for one and a quarter hours, entered a long hanging valley.

There we met a herd of buffaloes, though the valley floor was covered with snow very nearly to its mouth. On one of the first snow-slopes was collected a thick crowd of vultures—a strange spectacle; in a few minutes the explanation of it came into view in the shape of a dead buffalo. This was altogether too much for the Gurkhas, who picked up half a dozen stones apiece and raced off to the assault, while we sat down and, substituting cold mutton for buffalo, proceeded to do pretty much what the vultures had been doing. It was funny to see them now, hopping up the snow with wings outspread; but, ungainly as their movements were, they kept out of range of their nimble assailants with absolute ease.

The rest of the glen was indescribably dreary and desolate. At its head rose an uninteresting mountain, in very bad repair, which bowled down biggish stones with remarkable regularity at intervals of five or ten minutes. I took a violent dislike to this peak, and was shocked when Bruce pronounced it to be Shikara. The way lay to the right of it, up interminable hard gritty slopes just not too steep to walk on, than which I know nothing more boring and more tiring. The caravan straggled over these disgracefully, and at 3.30, among the very last of the coolies, I arrived at the col, fagged and cross, and, as usual, very hungry.

In his all too brief account of the visit to Khagan in 1896 Bruce has described an amusing incident in the passage of the first of his two cols. They found on reaching the top of the pass on the Khagan side a steep slope of hard frozen snow for about fifty feet, and then another fifty feet still steeper and harder, and foresaw trouble with the Khagani coolies.

"However," he says, "we hit upon a very good plan, which answered admirably; we stretched our only rope from the top down the first steep slope, cutting large steps right up to the edge of the ice-slope. At the edge we cut an immense step—the men had not been allowed to look over all this time and so were in ignorance of what was before them. One Gurkha was stationed on the top with the rope, one at the big step, and myself and Kharbir hardened our hearts and glissaded, sitting, on to the snow slope below. On the word being given a coolie was passed down with his load and made to sit on the big step; a violent push did the rest, and we did the fielding at the bottom."

But when I joined Bruce on the col I was met by

the announcement, "Je me suis trompé," so I had a look round. We were in a well-defined rocky gap, between a ridge running down from Shikara and a spur belonging to another rock peak on the right which had only recently come into view. It was a beautiful col, but it was certainly not the scene of the Khaganis' involuntary sitting glissade. Icy slopes fell away in front of us with startling abruptness for some hundreds of feet to a small glacier below, embraced by a rib projecting from Shikara—if, indeed, it was Shikara, for its title to that name had been considerably shaken. In the centre, below the middle of the gap, the slope soon turned into actual glacier, and was quite impassable; but Inderbinen and the Gurkhas had already been busy for some time at the side, hugging the rocks of the right-hand peak and cutting steps of the soup-plate order. Fifty or sixty feet below the col there was a conveniently shaped stone tightly frozen in; all the rope we possessed, probably 150 to 200 feet, was got out and fastened to the stone, over which Jeman Sing squatted, while Inderbinen took up a position by the bergschrund—which, luckily, was not a big one—at the bottom of the steepest bit, and took charge of the other end.

It was decidedly the most awkward place that we took coolies over—not so dangerous as the traverse into the Rishi valley, but very much more difficult. The Kashmiris, with a single exception, faced it with admirable pluck, and went down steadily and well. One of them only remained tearful and shivering at the top. Bruce took off a scarf he was wearing, knotted it loosely round the man's waist, and holding one end in his hand bade the waverer go forward, for all would be well. It was a remarkable illustration of the value of "moral support"; he started off at once quite cheerful and confident, and all were safe at the bottom of the slope a few minutes later.

The topographical situation—which became perfectly clear in the course of the next morning—was as

follows:—The Batta Kundi nala, in which we now were, runs up from the main Khagan valley in a south-westerly direction, and we had entered it at right angles to its course. It ends in the elevated snow-field crossed by Bruce in 1896, from which a glacier descends just far enough to join the one below our pass. The first of Bruce's two cols was on the other side of the pseudo Shikara, and the true Shikara rose between the two at the very head of the valley. The second col led into the Safa Mula nala, where Dina was to meet us. We had seen it from our own pass, but it was past five o'clock by the time we had completed our descent—far too late to think of crossing it—and we camped just below the two glaciers.

The 1896 route is probably both shorter and easier, but we were quite satisfied to have stumbled upon a new and amusing little pass. We ought also to

have had a fine view of the south-eastern face of Mali, but fully half of the mountain was wrapped in dense clouds. I should say, from a very imperfect inspection, that the ascent of it from that side, if possible at all, would be an immensely long and arduous business.

The day ended with a violent snowstorm. I cannot in the least recollect whether there was any fuel within reach—that hardly seems possible—or whether we had brought some along as a precautionary measure; I only know that Kar Sing, a servant of Bruce's who had taken Dina's place, rose sublimely to the occasion and escorted me under an immense umbrella to Bruce's tent, where we were regaled on a princely dinner of pea-soup and a great many fried eggs.

The succeeding morning was cloudless, but so intensely cold that, contrary to all precedent, we breakfasted indoors, and then loitered awhile so as to start in the sun. It was about one and a half hours' actual walking to the second col; but we took things very easily, photographing and studying the arête which descended towards us from Shikara, and up which lay the obvious route to the summit.

The scenery had somewhat disappointed me on the previous day, but now I changed my mind about it entirely, and was inclined to class it with the view of the head of the Zinal valley from the Mountet hut, though the scale of heights and distances is considerably smaller; and Mali, the only peak worthy to be pitted against the Dent Blanche, unfortunately does not come into the picture. The false Shikara was transformed into a massive and stately cone, and the rocky mass on the other side of yesterday's pass presented an unexpectedly fine show of buttresses, holding between them deep gullies of snow, and broken by a deep rent which looked obtrusively like another pass, considerably higher than ours, and leading, possibly, back into the head of the glen above Tod Galli. Above all, we were fascinated by the graceful symmetry of Shikara, a dazzling white pyramid rising from the centre of the broad expanse of spotless snow.

Inderbinen was eager to stop where we were, and attack Shikara on the following day; but Bruce, before anything was attempted, wished to get his letters and to make sure of Dina. We were some days overdue, and he started the distressing theory that Dina had got tired of waiting and gone back, and began to hold forth with aggravating cheerfulness on the merits of the dak bungalow at Narang. It was like inviting some one who had been anticipating a night at Randa to wax enthusiastic over an hotel at Brieg.

An hour after leaving the col we were down at the base of Mali, which soared up 5000 or 6000 feet above us, but we were too close under it to get much impression of height, or to be able to form any satisfactory judgment as to the proper way up. On the stony floor of the valley there were a few tenantless huts and a stray horse or two, but no other signs of life, so we trudged on for two hours more, passing a small lake and scarcely descending at all, nearly to the mouth of the valley, which ends with a long steep drop to the level of the Kunhar river.

Here, if anywhere, we might expect to find Dina, and here, to my great relief, we did find him, abundantly supplied with all necessaries and a good many luxuries, amongst them several ducks and a goose. The ducks fulfilled their destiny in due time, but the goose wandered off somewhere that night, on an exploring expedition, and was never seen again.

We had proposed to devote ourselves, in the first instance, to Mali, but a tremendous storm upset all plans and calculations. Fresh snow was lying within 800 feet of the camp next morning, and Mali was literally smothered in it. For a day or two nothing could be done, and a general break-up of the weather seemed not unlikely ; it was decided to try and make sure of Shikara if possible. The whole camp was moved up to the foot of Mali on the 20th, and the ominous fact was noted that the whole of that side of the mountain remained entirely sunless till half-past ten. On the

21st we returned with a light kit to pass No. 2, and camped there.

The weather looked very doubtful, and snow fell during the night, but the morning of September 22 broke fine, though the cold, till the sun reached the col at about seven o'clock, was stinging. At 7.30 Bruce, Inderbinen, and I, with Pahal Sing and Jeman Sing, started for Shikara. We got down to the edge of the snow plateau in six or seven minutes, put on the rope, and walked briskly across to the foot of the peak, which was reached at 8.45. The small bergschrund gave no trouble, and we were sitting on the rocks at the foot of the arête before nine. By now the sun was fairly powerful, and we were hot and perspiring, but still I was a little surprised to see Inderbinen deposit his gloves, scarf, and second waistcoat under a stone before we started again.

After that it was a matter of continuously steep straightforward climbing for about three hours; Inderbinen led in good style, but there was not much choice of route; big bits of slabby rock were encountered every now and then that were not exactly easy, but no serious check occurred. Being five on one rope, we went slowly, and the whole ascent would have been simpler and quicker but for the large quantity of fresh snow. The only part there was ever any doubt about was the snowy bit at the top of the arête, which was narrow and extremely steep. There was no question of the possibility of getting up it, but I should not have cared to trust everybody's judgment as to what it would be like coming down. However, Inderbinen showed unwavering confidence on this point, and, keen as he was on leading a party on a successful first ascent, he was not the man to let his ardour run away with him.

A pretty little terrace of snow led round to the summit at 12.40. Bruce was the only member of the party who had previously taken part in the ascent of a virgin peak, and we all enjoyed a comfortable feeling of elation. The Gurkhas were frankly delighted, and eager to be photographed on the top.

Shikara is almost certainly the second peak in the

Khagan chain, and rises in the very centre of it, but I cannot conscientiously say that the view, as a whole, was very remarkable. The crowd of Rajee Bojee peaks stretched southward in unimpressive confusion; clouds had rolled up in the north, and Nanga Parbat was invisible. The one imposing object in the panorama was the dark mass of Mali. Seen from this elevation it rose above its ridge majestically, square and solid as a Norman keep, crowned by a lesser rock tower which formed the summit, and overtopped us by seven or eight hundred feet. There is plenty of good climbing in the rest of the range, but all on a moderate scale: Mali alone is a veritable giant, and whoever succeeds in conquering it will have won a big mountaineering prize.

It was here that we finally determined to abandon the attempt to secure it ourselves. For after the first half-hour of the ascent of the arête we had all suffered acutely from the cold; it had come as a complete surprise to everybody, especially to Inderbinen. We were already thoroughly warm; the hour was ten o'clock to twelve; the sun had shone brightly throughout, and only the gentlest of breezes had blown occasionally; but it was just about as much as one could stand.

To make an assault on Mali would mean a start with the temperature below zero, and no chance of getting into the sun for many hours, while it was certain that some of the climbing would be difficult and slow. None of us had any stomach for such a fight: Inderbinen pronounced with great decision that no hands could hold out at it for half an hour, and no one was inclined to contradict him.

THE KHAGAN RANGE FROM THE PIR-KA-DER PASS.

THE KHAGAN RANGE FROM THE PIR-KA-DER PASS.

We consoled ourselves with the reflection that time was slipping by, and what was left at our disposal would have only sufficed for a single attempt; and that, probably, at least two would be required before a way to the summit was found; but, setting that consideration aside altogether, I have no doubt that we decided rightly, and that for this particular expedition we were some weeks too late.

The descent required care, but the snow, as Inderbinen had predicted, behaved well. We were off the arête by 4.15, and at half-past five regained the little camp on the col, where it was decided to spend another night. We could have easily regained the main camp that evening if necessary, indeed we could have quite well made the whole expedition from it, but it would have involved facing two or three hours of intense cold, which we almost entirely escaped. If you are climbing for pleasure, camp high and start late.

## CHAPTER XVIII

### THE LAST STAGE

ON September 24 we started to work our way in and out over the spurs running down towards the Kunhar river. This was the last stage of the journey, and it began by an ascent, direct from the camping-place at the foot of Mali, of the ridge which encloses the Safa Mula nala on the southern side. Dina returned to the main valley by the way he had come, with the mules and the heavy baggage.

The top of the ridge was reached in two hours, and I was fortunate enough to obtain a fine panorama from the pass—which Bruce named the Pir-ka-Der pass—extending from Mali to a snowy hump called Nila, near the southern extremity of the icy portion of the Khagan range. The whole of the southern face of Mali was in full view, tremendously steep, and much exposed to a raking fire of stones and of ice avalanches from the patches of glacier which lay in the folds of the rocky slopes. The western arête appeared to present no serious difficulties, if it could be reached, but the direct way from the ridge was barred by a cut-off of unusual sharpness. One often hears of perpendicular precipices, but very seldom sees them; this one, where it was seen in profile, appeared not merely to be sheer, but actually to overhang, and a study of the photographs has since confirmed the impression. We could not make out any certain way of getting to the arête above this obstacle; whether there was any means of turning it on the other side was, of course, only a matter of speculation. On

the whole, our examination of the mountain confirmed the conclusion which we had already arrived at, that the likeliest route to the summit was from the east.

Shikara rose up finely in the centre of the panorama —it may fairly be regarded as the hub of the Khagan range; from it and the snowy plateau at its foot the main chain, north and south, the ridge on which we were standing, and the ridge from which Mali rises radiate like the spokes of a wheel.

On the far side of our ridge lies the Manur glen, which runs parallel with the main Kunhar valley for many miles before joining it, resembling in this respect that of the Jagran river on the other side of the chain, except that it does not extend so far to the north. The head of the principal arm lay immediately below us ; a lesser one branches off lower down, and runs up to the southern base of Shikara. Most of the descent lay through a steepish gully full of old avalanche snow, down which we got some roughish glissades ; at the bottom of the gully, which is so much shut in that the sun can have but little effect upon it, the snow has solidified into regular glacier ice, hard and blue, with a small crevasse in it. I have read a description of a similar phenomenon in the gorge of the Limmernbach above Stachelberg, but have never seen anything like it before. The snow continued to cover in the stream for some distance after the valley floor was reached, and here the Gurkhas had a great triumph. They had been "putting" large stones on to the snow at intervals, and one of them placed an unusually big one on to exactly the right spot, at what one is tempted to call the psychological moment, with the result that a mighty mass, over twenty yards in length by six or seven yards broad, collapsed into the water. Not long after this episode we reached the forest, and a beautiful camping-ground ; but in the Kashmir and Khagan valleys below the tree-level one takes beautiful camping-grounds as a matter of course.

Next day's march was a long tramp down the Manur glen. At the principal village everybody seemed to

A VILLAGE IN KASHMIR.

know Bruce, and we held a regular Durbar on the roof of the largest house. These roofs are a great feature both in Khagan and in the Kishenganga valley; the houses for the most part are built against the slope of the hill, in such wise that the flat roof is easily accessible from behind. Bruce propounded the theory that they built their houses in this fashion because otherwise they would not have any flat places at all; and certainly the uses to which they put the roofs give him considerable support. Tents are pitched on them occasionally, and stacks of hay and grain are placed upon them very frequently; I have seen a man on horseback select a house-top as a halting-place when he wanted to get off his horse and rest, and they seem to be the invariable place used for purposes of assemblage and conversation.

One of our visitors on this occasion was a man who claimed to be 120 years old, and was admitted on all hands to have passed the century. He was quite toothless, but full of life and vigour, and age had not dimmed the brightness of his hawk-like eyes. His recollection went back beyond the time of Ranjit Singh, and the British raj was the fifth under which he had lived. He was very curious as to what my business was, and when he was told that I had come to see the beauties of the country, his keen old eyes beamed on me with approval.

As we were leaving the village we caught sight of the blue waters of a small lake, the appearance of which caused Bruce considerable surprise. On inquiry, it appeared that it was the result of a landslip which had occurred only two months before; we passed it a few minutes later and saw half-submerged trees showing above the surface, like the melancholy palms of Philæ. A tongue of earth and stones extended across the valley, forming a dam below the lake, and partially covering several maize-fields. Eight or ten houses had been destroyed, and there must have been some narrow escapes, but only a single life was lost.

We came to a halt two or three miles farther on, where the valley is joined by the long, narrow wooded Bichla glen, which descends from the heart of the chain, and to the head of which we ascended on the following day. Most of the able-bodied men were high up in the hills with cattle, or busy getting in the hay and crops, and there was some trouble in mustering a sufficient number of porters: some of them were very decrepit, and the pace was accordingly slow, but leisurely progress was pleasant through the beautiful scenery, which awoke vague far-away memories of the Schyn pass.

The valley ends in a fine wall of jagged rock, broken by a broad gap filled with glacier; on either hand sharp teeth and steep towers give promise of short but interesting climbs, and the opening is a really striking pass. It seems to correspond with the Bichla pass of the map, across which a zigzag track is marked; Bruce, however, named it the Jagran pass, and said that it had not been crossed, so far as he was aware. It was just the kind of place that a mountaineering party could get natives over, but that natives would not be likely to use themselves. All that I know about the other side of it is that there is an immensely long descent to the Jagran river, which has here descended far below the level of the Tod Galli plateau. It was this feature of it which decided us against the idea, in itself attractive, of trying to cross the pass and find a way back over the chain lower down. Instead of doing so we kept to the western side, and leaving the Bichla valley, found ourselves near the snowy dome of Nila, which had been a conspicuous object in the view from the Pir-ka-Der pass.

Inderbinen and I walked up it—it is a simple walk, mostly over easy snow-slopes—while the rest of the caravan skirted its base in a southerly direction. The top is decorated by a very large and solid cairn, built years ago by surveyors, and the detour to it was well worth making for the sake of the distant views, though the interesting part of the range appears to end with the peaks at the head of the Bichla glen, and the expanse of snow-field immediately around us was featureless.

Plunging straight down the face we rejoined, in a quarter of an hour, the broad track made by the caravan through the snow, and this was our farewell—rather a tame one—to the Indian ice-world. We reached a ragged rocky gap, and found ourselves looking into the head of one of the branches of the Bhunja valley. The caravan, now nearly at the bottom, were resting on a grassy spur, and looked as though one could have easily thrown a biscuit on to their heads; it was a wild-looking place, ending in a fine cirque of brown precipices, which were crowned on the far side by one or two small glaciers—the very last.

On September 28 we walked down to the junction of the two arms of the Bhunja valley, and crossed another ridge, and then, after five days' steady travelling, I was very ready for a rest before starting for our last bit of climbing, the ascent of Makra.

Makra (12,749 feet), with which the mountainous part of the Khagan range comes to an end, is a notable hill, very conspicuous from the Jhelam valley road. Owing to its situation it commands a remarkable panorama, but I was already familiar with the views to the north and west, and had seen them to equal or greater advantage elsewhere; what was novel and delightful was the prospect to the south, where the Kishenganga and the Jhelam converge, and the mountains fall away into low spurs and ridges, clothed with rich and luxuriant vegetation. We looked across the vast spaces of this green hollow at the heights of the

Kaj Nag, where Bruce had had a curious experience in the course of a shooting trip some years before; he came upon a stretch of ground deeply covered with innumerable dead locusts, which had been caught and killed by the wind, like those we had seen near Wan; and nine bears were busily engaged in making a meal off them.

Beyond Makra the range dwindles down to a single narrow ridge, along which we started for our last march on October 1st. It is so sharp in places that there is barely room for a path, and one looks down simultaneously on the waters of the Kunhar, the Jhelam, and the Kishenganga. Our circuit was completed; we were not more than fourteen miles from Domel on the road from Rawal Pindi, through which we had driven just six weeks before.

I hope I have made it clear that to have seen the Khagan range (not quite "from End to End," but very nearly so) under Bruce's auspices and guidance was a very enviable experience; a more enjoyable finish to a trip in the Himalaya it would be hard to imagine. Any one driven from other regions by the advent of the rains could not well do better than follow in our footsteps; while if Johnson's idea of a Himalayan Alpine Club is ever revived, its members will find in Khagan an ideal training-ground. Good rock climbs are numerous, and the snow and ice work is not too formidable; there is an interesting bit of original research to be done in the district north of Tod Galli and our pass of September 17; and Mali is still, alas! unattempted.

Yet I cannot but recognise that this region, in spite of its many merits, is no more likely than Haramukh to receive much attention from parties coming out from England for many years to come. The giant peaks will exert their potent attraction, just as Mont Blanc did—to a degree which people nowadays have almost forgotten—on earlier climbers, and the struggle to break the altitude record will continue—who can say how long? The day of the lesser ranges has not yet come; I am glad that a happy series of chances led me to visit one of them out of due season.

One more night in camp, and then down to the Kunhar river at Gari Habibulla. Here were an excellent road, a telegraph, and a dak bungalow; in a word, civilisation once more. I found an ancient bound volume of the *Athenæum*, and read with absorbing zest and interest reviews of Clarence King's *Mountaineering in the Sierra Nevada* and *Good-bye, Sweetheart, Good-bye.* Just behind Gari Habibulla there is a depression in the hills on the west of the Kunhar, over which lies the natural route for the railway to Kashmir, if it ever comes into being. We reached the little pass on October 8 by one of Bruce's short-cuts; vehicles were waiting for us on the other side, and late in the evening we drove into Abbottabad.

There, with a clear conscience and amid most encouraging surroundings, I spent a week of glorious idleness. The Gurkhas got up a dance for my special benefit; I made the acquaintance of that great mountaineer Harkir, and had the satisfaction of personally expressing the thanks of our party to Colonel Kemball. Then, back to the plains once more. As I wandered later amongst the splendours of Delhi and Agra, the memory of life in the mountains became remote and dream-like, and my only link with the past was the excellent Dina, whose services Bruce kindly placed at my disposal. During a month of visits and sight-seeing he looked after me with boundless zeal and a very fair amount of discretion, and, on November 9, saw me safely embarked at Bombay.

THE END

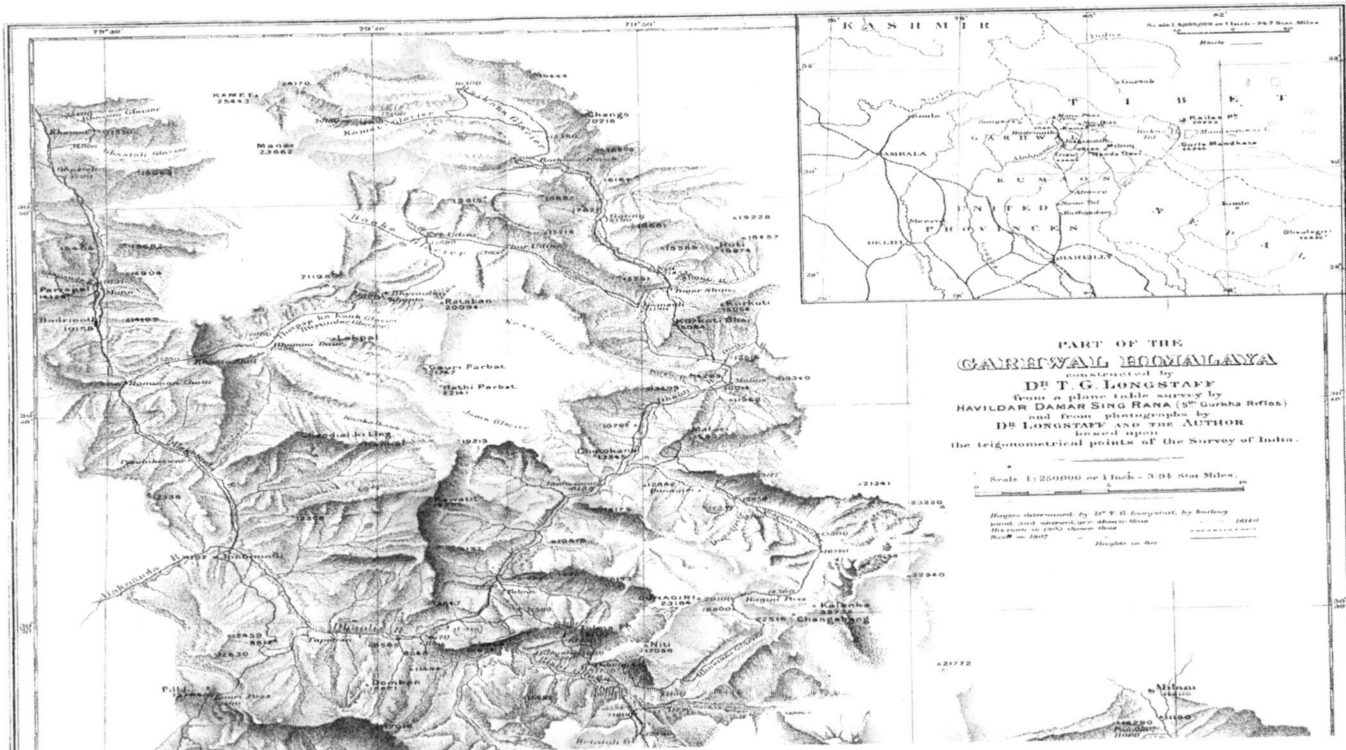
PART OF THE
GARHWAL HIMALAYA
constructed by
Dr. T. G. LONGSTAFF
from a plane table survey by
HAVILDAR DAMAR SING RANA (5th Gurkha Rifles)
and from photographs by
Dr. LONGSTAFF AND THE AUTHOR
based upon
the trigonometrical points of the Survey of India.
Scale 1:250000 or 1 Inch = 3.94 Stat Miles.
Heights in feet
KASHMIR
TIBET
GARHWAL
KUMAON
UNITED PROVINCES
AMBALA
BAREILLY
KAMET
25443
Mana
23862
Chango
20716
Ratabon
20094
Gauri Parbat
Hathi Parbat
22141
Niti
Kalanka
Changabang
Milam
Badrinath
Joshimath
Alaknanda

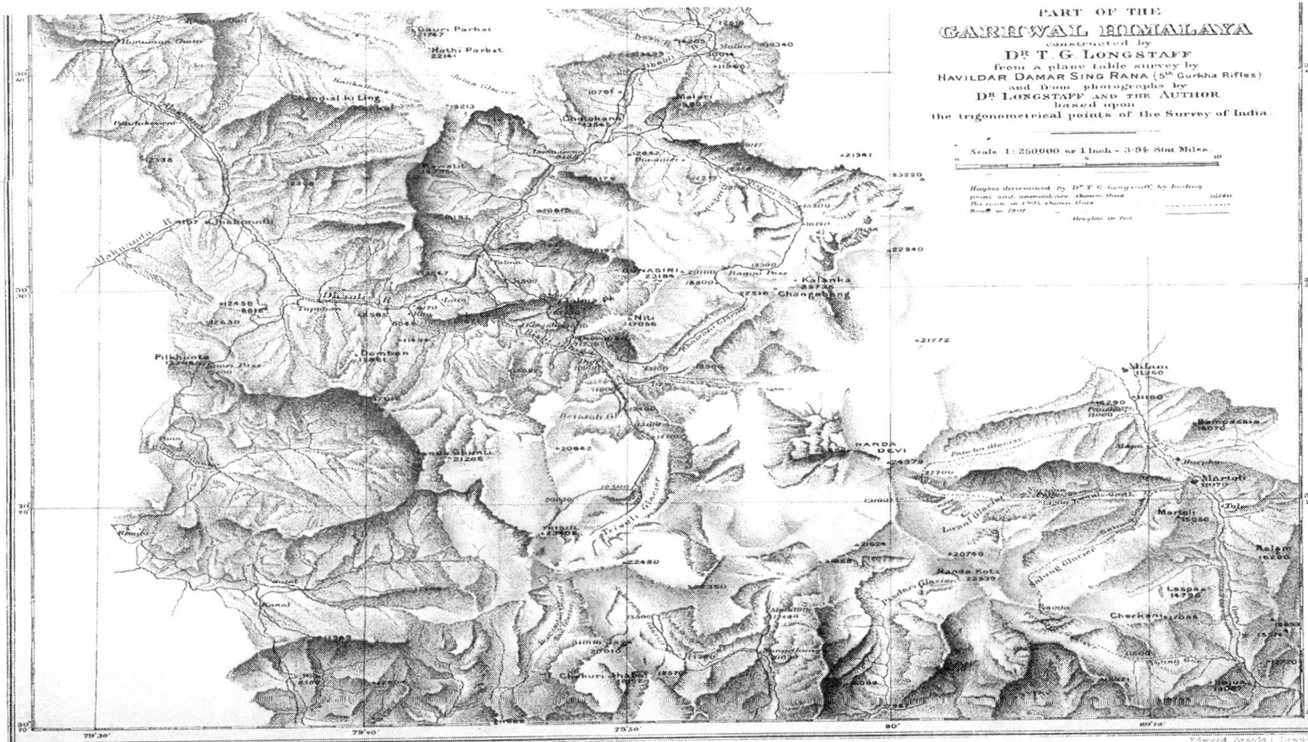
PART OF THE
GARHWAL HIMALAYA
constructed by
Dr. T. G. LONGSTAFF
from a plane table survey by
HAVILDAR DAMAR SING RANA (5th Gurkha Rifles)
and from photographs by
Dr. LONGSTAFF AND THE AUTHOR
based upon
the trigonometrical points of the Survey of India.
Scale 1 : 250,000 or 1 Inch = 3·94 Stat Miles.
Heights in feet
Gauri Parbat
21747
Hathi Parbat
22141
Joshimath
Dhauli R.
Tapoban
Pilkhunta
Dunagiri
23184
Kalanka
Changabang
NANDA DEVI
Nanda Ghunti
21286
Trisul
Trisuli Glacier
Bagini Pass
Milam
Martoli
Nanda Kot
22530
Ralam
Laspa
Cherkani
Chakuri Shakti
79°30′
79°40′
79°50′
80°
80°10′
Edward Arnold : London

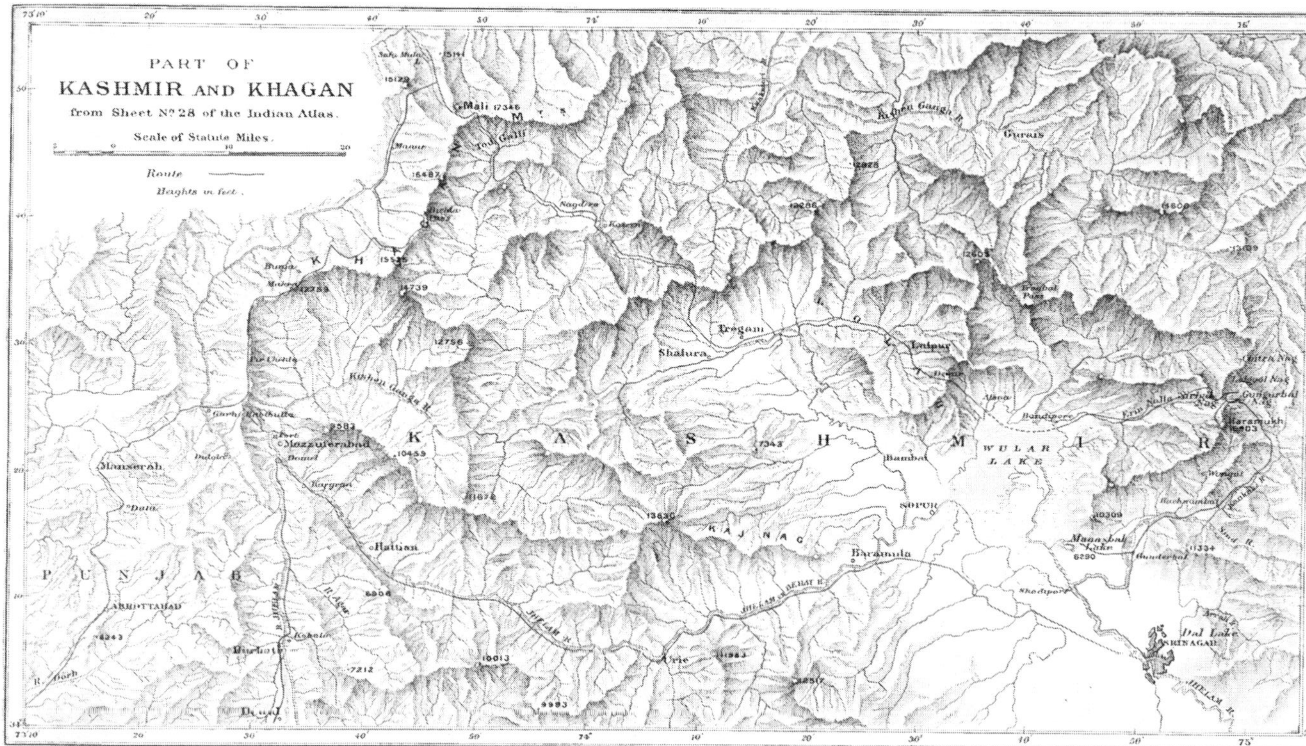
PART OF
KASHMIR AND KHAGAN
from Sheet No. 28 of the Indian Atlas.
Scale of Statute Miles.
Route
Heights in feet.
Mali 17346
Gurais
Tregam
Shalura
Lalpur
WULAR LAKE
Bandipore
Bambai
SOPUR
Baramula
Manasbal Lake
Shadipore
Dal Lake
SRINAGAR
JHELAM R.
Mozufferabad
Hattian
Uric
Mansehra
PUNJAB
ABBOTTABAD
KASHMIR
KAJ NAG
Haramukh
Gungurbal Nag
Chitra Nag
London, Edward Arnold

# INDEX

# INDEX

## INDEX